Digital Marketing

The Success Guide to Mastering Strategy, Use of AI, and Building a Profitable Customer Base

Waldo's Publishing Company

WALDO'S PUBLISHING
EST
2024
COMPANY

Contents

Introduction

Digital marketing can often feel like trying to navigate a maze blindfolded. You're bombarded with terms like SEO, PPC, and AI, and it's easy to feel overwhelmed. Business owners and beginners alike face common hurdles: staying updated with fast-changing trends, knowing where to invest time and money, and getting measurable results. Did you know that 50% of small businesses don't have a digital marketing strategy? That's leaving a lot of potential growth on the table.

So, let's simplify things.

This book serves as a comprehensive guide to digital marketing, incorporating the latest AI tools while avoiding complex industry language. Whether you're experienced or just beginning, it aims to make digital marketing accessible to everyone. Consider it a roadmap for growing a successful business using effective online strategies. You'll find actionable tactics ready for use, along with real-world case studies to illustrate what works and what doesn't. By the end of the book, you'll have a complete set of strategies to improve your business's online presence and profitability.

Here's a quick look at what's inside:

- **Developing a Digital Marketing Strategy**: We'll start with the basics. How to create a strategy that aligns with your business goals.

- **Leveraging AI Technologies**: Learn how to use AI to optimize your marketing efforts. From chatbots to personalized emails, AI is a game-changer.

- **Social Media Marketing**: Discover the best practices for platforms like Facebook, Instagram, LinkedIn, and Twitter. Learn how to engage your audience and build a loyal following.

- **Email Marketing**: Dive into strategies for creating effective email campaigns that convert.

- **Data Analytics**: Understand how to measure your success. Learn what metrics to track and how to interpret them.

- **Future-Proofing Your Strategy**: Stay ahead of the curve with tips for adapting to future trends and technologies.

So, dive into this book and transform your digital marketing efforts. By the end of this journey, you will have a clear, actionable plan to create a profitable business through digital marketing. This isn't just theory; it's a practical guide designed to get you results.

Let's get started on this journey together. Your profitable digital marketing future begins now.

Chapter One

Building a Strong Foundation in Digital Marketing

You're not alone if you've ever felt lost in the digital marketing world. Many business owners and beginners face the same challenge. Here's a relatable scenario: You launch a website, create social media profiles, and maybe even send out a few emails. But then, nothing happens. Where are the customers? Where's the engagement? It's frustrating, right? The truth is, digital marketing isn't just about being online; it's about being strategic. This chapter is all about laying down that solid foundation so you can finally see the results you've been dreaming of.

Understanding Digital Marketing Basics

Let's start with the basics. Digital marketing, in simple terms, is the promotion of products or services through digital channels like search engines, social media, email, and websites. Unlike traditional marketing, which relies on physical applications like print ads and billboards, digital marketing uses online platforms to reach consumers. This shift has been monumental. When Yahoo launched in 1994, it got a million hits in its first year, which was a massive deal back then. Fast-forward to today, and Google processes over 3.5 billion searches per day. That's the power of the internet.

So, how does digital marketing differ from traditional marketing? Traditional marketing is often broad and less targeted. Think of a TV commercial or a newspaper ad; it reaches a wide audience, but you can't control who sees it. Digital marketing, on the other hand, allows for precise targeting. You can reach specific demographics based on age, location, interests, and behavior. This makes your marketing efforts more efficient and cost-effective.

This is why a digital presence is crucial for businesses today. According to Forbes, 85% of consumers conduct online research before making a purchase. If your business isn't online, you're missing out on a massive chunk of potential customers. A strong digital presence helps you communicate with consumers, set narratives, and differentiate from competitors. Plus, it's cost-effective. The digital advertising industry is valued at around $200 billion, but you don't need a huge budget to get started. Even small investments can yield significant returns.

Digital marketing offers numerous benefits. It's measurable, allowing you to track performance and adjust strategies in real-time. It's scalable, meaning you can start small and grow your efforts as your business expands. Moreover, it's interactive, enabling direct engagement with your audience. The key channels in digital marketing include SEO (Search Engine Optimization), PPC (Pay-Per-Click) advertising, social media marketing, email marketing, and content marketing. Each channel has its unique strengths and can be leveraged to achieve different goals.

The Digital Marketing Ecosystem

Think of the digital marketing ecosystem as a well-oiled machine with several moving parts. These parts consist of your website, content, customer journey, and data and analytics.

At the heart of this ecosystem is your website. Your website serves as the central hub for all your digital marketing activities. It's where you drive traffic, convert leads, and provide valuable information to visitors. Ensuring it's user-friendly, mobile-responsive, and optimized for search engines is key.

Content is the foundation of digital marketing. Whether it's blog posts, videos, infographics, or social media updates, content is how you communicate with your audience. It helps build trust, establish authority, and drive engagement. Quality content tailored to your audience's interests and needs can significantly impact your digital marketing success.

The customer journey in digital marketing involves multiple touchpoints. Prospective customers might first encounter your brand through a social media post, then visit your website, sign up for your newsletter, and finally make a purchase after reading a few blog posts. Understanding this journey helps you create a seamless experience that guides prospects from awareness to conversion.

Data and analytics are the backbone of effective digital marketing. They provide insights into what's working and what's not, enabling you to make informed decisions. Tools like Google Analytics help track website performance, user behavior, and campaign effectiveness. By analyzing this data, you can refine your strategies and improve results over time.

Key Digital Marketing Metrics

To measure your digital marketing performance, you need to track specific metrics.

- Traffic metrics, such as visitors and page views, indicate how many people are visiting your site.

- Engagement metrics, like bounce rate and average session duration, show how users interact with your content.

- Conversion metrics, including conversion rate and cost per acquisition, measure how effectively your marketing efforts turn visitors into customers.

- Return on investment (ROI) and customer lifetime value (CLV), help you understand the financial impact of your marketing activities.

Key Digital Marketing Terminology Explained

Let's break down some of the most common terms you'll encounter in digital marketing. We'll start with **SEO**, or Search Engine Optimization. SEO involves improving your website so that it ranks higher on search engine results pages (**SERPs**). Imagine you're a bakery in New York. When someone Googles "best bakery in New York," SEO helps ensure your bakery shows up near the top. This process involves tweaking your website content, using the right keywords, and building backlinks. It's a long-term strategy that drives organic traffic—visitors who find you through unpaid search results.

Next up is **PPC**, or Pay-Per-Click advertising. Unlike SEO, which focuses on organic traffic, PPC generates immediate traffic through paid ads. You've seen those ads at the top of Google search results marked as "Ad." That's PPC in action. Advertisers bid on keywords, and they pay each time someone clicks on their ad. It's a quick way to get in front of potential customers. For instance, if you're launching a new product and want instant visibility, a well-planned PPC campaign can drive traffic to your site immediately.

CTR, or Click-Through Rate, is another crucial term. It measures the percentage of people who click on your ad or link out of the total who see it. For example, if 100 people see your ad and 10 click on it, your CTR is 10%. It's an important metric because a higher CTR indicates that your ad is relevant and compelling to your audience. It's like having a billboard that makes people pull over to check out your store instead of just driving by.

Finally, the **Conversion Rate** measures how many visitors complete a desired action on your site. This could be making a purchase, filling out a contact form, or signing up for a newsletter . If 10,000 people visit your site and 500 make a purchase, your conversion rate is 5%. It's the ultimate indicator of your marketing effectiveness. High traffic is great, but it's the conversions that pay the bills. Think of it as the percentage of window shoppers who actually buy something.

Why is each term important? SEO drives organic traffic. Without it, your site is like a shop in an alley with no signposts. PPC campaigns generate immediate traffic, offering a quick return on investment. CTR helps you to understand the effectiveness of your ads, ensuring you're spending money wisely. Conversion Rate, meanwhile, tells you how well your site turns visitors into customers. Together, these metrics form the pillars of a robust digital marketing strategy.

The Role of SEO in Your Digital Strategy

Search Engine Optimization (SEO) serves as the foundation for digital marketing. It's the art and science of getting your website to rank higher on search engines like Google. Imagine it as the digital version of setting up your shop on the busiest street in town.

When someone searches for a product or service that you offer, you want your website to be one of the first they see. This visibility can drive significant organic traffic, meaning people find you without paid ads. SEO is divided into two main categories: on-page and off-page. On-page SEO involves optimizing elements on your website itself, like content and HTML code. Off-page SEO focuses on building backlinks from other websites to boost your site's authority.

Keyword research is fundamental to SEO. It involves identifying the words and phrases that potential customers use to find products or services like yours. Tools such as Google Keyword Planner and SEMrush are valuable for discovering relevant keywords. Once you have a list, you can integrate these keywords into your titles, content, and meta descriptions. This improves your chances of ranking higher in search results. But remember, keyword stuffing, cramming too many keywords into your content, can hurt your rankings. The important thing is to incorporate keywords naturally and within the appropriate context.

Content plays a crucial role in SEO. High-quality and relevant content attracts visitors and keeps them engaged. Search engines like Google reward websites that provide valuable information to users. This means regular blog posts, articles, and updates can significantly boost your SEO efforts. For instance, a local bakery might write blog posts about baking tips, recipes, and the history of their craft. This not only engages readers but also incorporates keywords naturally, improving search rankings.

On-page SEO techniques are your first line of defense in the battle for search engine rankings. Start with title tags and meta descriptions. The title tag is the headline that appears in search results, and the meta description is a brief summary underneath it. Both should be compelling and include your primary keyword. Header tags (H1, H2, H3) help structure your content, making it easier for search engines and users to understand. H1 is usually the main title, while H2 and H3 are subheadings. Internal linking is another powerful on-page tactic. Linking to other pages on your website enhances search engine crawling efficiency and encourages visitors to stay on your site longer. Finally, don't forget image optimization. Use descriptive file names and alternative (alt) text to make your images searchable.

Off-page SEO focuses on establishing authority and building trust for your website. One of the most effective ways to do this is through backlinks, links from other reputable websites to yours. Guest blogging is a popular strategy. Write valuable content for another site in exchange for a backlink. Social media engagement can also drive traffic and build links. Share your content on platforms like Facebook, Twitter, and LinkedIn to increase visibility. Influencer outreach is another tactic. Partner with influencers who can share your content with their audience, generating valuable backlinks in the process. Creating shareable content, like infographics and videos, can naturally attract links from other sites.

Measuring SEO success is crucial for understanding what's working and what needs improvement. Google Analytics is a powerful tool that tracks website traffic, user behavior, and more. It helps you see how visitors are finding your site and what they do once they're there. Google Search Console provides insights into your search performance, showing which keywords you rank for and how often your site appears in search results. Keyword ranking tools like SEMrush or Ahrefs track your rankings for specific keywords over time. Backlink analysis tools, such as Moz's Link Explorer, help you see who's linking to your site and assess the quality of those links.

SEO might seem complex, but breaking it down into these manageable components makes it easier to tackle. Understanding the fundamentals and implementing these strategies can significantly improve your online visibility and drive more organic traffic to your site.

Introduction to PPC Advertising

Pay-Per-Click (PPC) advertising is a model where advertisers pay a fee each time someone clicks on their ad. Essentially, it involves purchasing visits to your site rather than gathering them organically. Imagine putting up a billboard in a prime location but only paying for it when someone actually walks into your store because they saw it. That's the beauty of PPC. It's efficient and measurable. The way PPC auctions work is pretty straightforward. Advertisers bid on keywords relevant to their business. When someone searches for those keywords, an auction takes place in real-time. The search engine decides which ads to display based on factors like bid amount and ad quality. There are different types of PPC ads, including search ads that appear on search engine results pages, display ads on various websites, and social media ads on platforms like Facebook and Instagram.

Setting up a PPC campaign might seem daunting, but breaking it down into steps makes it manageable. First, choose the right platform. Google Ads is a popular option because of its extensive reach, but Bing Ads and social media platforms also offer valuable opportunities. Next, conduct keyword research. Tools like Google Keyword Planner can help you find relevant keywords with good search volume and manageable competition. Crafting compelling ad copy is crucial. Your ads should be concise but persuasive, highlighting what makes your offering unique. Include a strong call to action, like "Shop Now" or "Learn More." Then, set your budget and bid strategy. Decide how much you're willing to spend daily and how much you'll bid for each click. It's essential to balance between staying competitive and not overspending.

Once your campaign is live, optimization is key to maximizing ROI. Start with A/B testing your ad copy. Create different versions of your ads and test them to determine which one performs best. Analyzing and adjusting bids is also necessary. Monitor your campaigns regularly and adjust your bids based on performance. If certain keywords are driving conversions, consider increasing their bids. On the other side, lower bids for underperforming keywords. Negative keywords are another powerful tool. These are terms you don't want your ads to show for, helping you avoid irrelevant clicks. Lastly, focus on improving your Quality Score, which Google uses to gauge the relevance and quality of your ads. A higher Quality Score can lower your cost per click and improve ad placement. This score is influenced by factors like click-through rate, ad relevance, and landing page experience.

***

To illustrate the effectiveness of PPC, let's look at a real-world example.

A local electronics store wanted to boost online sales, so they decided to run a PPC campaign. Their primary objective was to increase sales of their new range of smart home devices. They started with Google Ads, targeting keywords like "buy smart thermostat" and "smart home security system." They crafted compelling ad copy highlighting discounts and free shipping. After setting a daily budget and bid strategy, they launched the campaign. The results were impressive. Within a month, they saw a 20% increase in online sales. Their ads had a high click-through rate, and their conversion rate was above industry average.

The key takeaway here is the importance of continuous optimization. They regularly analyzed their campaign performance, adjusted bids, and added negative keywords to refine their targeting. This iterative process significantly contributed to their success.

***

PPC advertising offers a powerful way to drive targeted traffic to your website quickly. By understanding the basics, setting up your campaigns strategically, and continuously optimizing, you can achieve impressive results. The ability to measure and adjust in real-time makes PPC an invaluable tool in any digital marketer's arsenal.

The Importance of Consistent Branding Online

Brand consistency might seem like a buzzword, but it's the foundation of any successful business. At its core, brand consistency is about ensuring that your brand's message, visuals, and tone remain uniform across all platforms and touchpoints. This uniformity helps build trust and recognition. Think of iconic brands like Coca-Cola and Apple. Coca-Cola's red and white color scheme, coupled with its classic font, is instantly recognizable worldwide. Similarly, Apple's sleek, minimalist design and consistent messaging about innovation and quality resonate across all its products and advertisements. Consistent branding fosters familiarity, and familiarity breeds trust. When customers trust a brand, they are more likely to engage and make purchases.

So, what are the key elements that contribute to brand consistency? First and foremost is the visual identity. This includes your logo, color scheme, and typography. These elements should be cohesive and reflect your brand's personality. For instance, a luxury brand might use elegant fonts and a sophisticated color palette, while a tech startup might opt for bold, modern visuals. Next, consider your brand voice and messaging. This is how you communicate with your audience. Is your tone formal or casual? Do you use humor or keep things serious? Consistency in voice ensures that your brand feels reliable and authentic. Content style and tone also play a significant role. Whether it's a blog post, social media update, or email newsletter, the style and tone should align with your brand identity. Lastly, the customer experience across touchpoints must be seamless. From your website to customer service interactions, every touchpoint should convey the same brand values and quality.

Creating a brand style guide is a practical way to ensure consistency. A brand style guide is a document that outlines the rules and guidelines for your brand's visual and verbal identity. It acts as a reference for anyone creating content for your brand, ensuring that everything is aligned. Key components of a brand style guide include the logo usage, color palette, typography, and imagery guidelines. It also covers the brand voice and tone, providing examples of do's and don'ts in communication. Implementing and enforcing a style guide requires regular training and communication with your team. Make sure everyone understands the importance of brand consistency and how to apply the guidelines in their work.

Mailchimp and Spotify have excellent brand style guides that are worth checking out. They offer clear, detailed guidelines that help maintain a cohesive brand identity across all platforms.

Measuring brand consistency is crucial for maintaining it over time. One effective method is conducting brand audits. A brand audit involves reviewing all your brand's touchpoints to ensure they align with your style guide. Look at your website, social media profiles, marketing materials, and even physical products. Customer feedback is another valuable tool. Regularly survey your customers to see if they perceive your brand consistently across different channels. Social media monitoring tools can help you track how your brand is being represented and discussed online. Finally, use consistency checklists for ongoing projects. These checklists ensure that every piece of content or marketing material meets your brand standards before it goes live.

In conclusion, consistent branding is not just a marketing tactic; it's a strategic necessity. It builds trust, fosters recognition, and creates a cohesive brand experience that resonates with customers. By focusing on visual identity, brand voice, content style, and customer experience, and by using tools like a brand style guide and regular audits, you can maintain a strong, consistent brand presence. This foundational consistency is what sets successful brands apart and keeps customers coming back.

Chapter Two

Creating Your Digital Marketing Strategy

I magine trying to build a house without a blueprint. You might end up with a wall where a window should be or a kitchen in the basement. This is what running a business without a digital marketing strategy feels like. You might be doing a lot, but without direction, it's hard to know if your efforts are paying off. A well-defined digital strategy serves as your roadmap, aligning marketing efforts with your business goals, ensuring efficient resource allocation, and maintaining consistency in messaging. It's like having a GPS for your business, guiding you to your destination while avoiding unnecessary detours.

Planning Your Strategy

A digital marketing plan is your strategic guide to achieving marketing goals. It coordinates different marketing efforts, ensuring that each activity supports the overall business objectives. Think of it as a symphony where every instrument, social media, email, SEO, plays its part in harmony. Without this coordination, you risk wasting resources on disjointed efforts that don't move the needle. A good plan provides a clear roadmap, helping you navigate the complex digital landscape while staying focused on your goals.

The core components of a solid digital marketing plan include a situation analysis, marketing goals and objectives, and target audience segmentation.

- Situation analysis, such as a SWOT analysis, to understand your strengths, weaknesses, opportunities, and threats. This sets the stage for identifying what you need to focus on.

- Marketing goals and objectives. These should be specific and measurable, like increasing website traffic by 20% in six months.

- Target audience is crucial. Segment your audience based on psychographics, demographics, and behaviors to tailor your messages effectively. For instance, if you're targeting young professionals, your tone and channels might differ from targeting retirees.

Budgeting and resource allocation are critical parts of your digital marketing plan. Allocate your budget efficiently by prioritizing high-impact activities. Target strategies that offer the best return on investment (ROI). For example, if social media ads have previously driven significant traffic and conversions, allocate more funds there. ROI-focused budgeting ensures you get the most bang for your buck. Estimate costs for different channels and tactics, allowing for flexibility and unexpected expenses. Regularly review your budget to adjust as needed based on campaign performance. Track spending using tools like QuickBooks or Excel to ensure you stay within budget while maximizing impact.

Monitoring and adjusting your digital marketing plan are ongoing processes. Regular performance reviews help you track progress against your goals. Use analytics tools to measure key metrics and identify what's working and what needs adjustment. Be flexible and adaptable, ready to pivot strategies based on data insights. Establish feedback loops for continuous improvement. Motivate team members to share their ideas, supporting a culture of ongoing optimization and growth. This process ensures your digital marketing efforts remain effective and aligned with your business goals.

Developing a digital strategy involves several key steps. Start by setting SMART goals. These goals provide clear direction and benchmarks for success. Next, identify your target audience. Conduct audience research using surveys, social media listening, and website analytics to understand their needs and preferences. Conduct a competitor analysis to see what's working for others in your industry. Pinpoint gaps and potential avenues to make your brand stand out. This comprehensive approach ensures your digital marketing strategy is well-rounded and poised for success.

Setting Clear and Achievable Marketing Goals

When you're planning your digital marketing efforts, it's crucial to set SMART goals. SMART stands for Specific, Measurable, Achievable, Relevant, and Time-bound. Imagine you want to "increase website traffic." That's a good start, but it's vague. Instead, aim for "increase website traffic by 20% in three months." This goal is specific and gives you a clear target. Measurable goals are vital because they allow you to track progress. Use tools like Google Analytics to monitor metrics such as traffic, conversion rates, and bounce rates. This way, you can see if you're on track or need to adjust your strategies.

Achievability is another key factor. Setting unrealistic goals can lead to frustration. Ensure your goals are achievable, considering your current resources and limitations. For instance, if your team is small, aiming to double your content output in a month might not be feasible. Instead, set a goal that stretches your capabilities but remains realistic. Aligning your goals with broader business objectives is also essential. If your company is launching a new product, your marketing goals should support this initiative. For example, you could aim to "generate 500 qualified leads for the new product launch by Q3 2023." This ensures your marketing efforts are relevant and contribute to overall business success.

Being time-bound adds urgency and focus to your goals. Set deadlines for achieving them. For instance, "achieve a 20% increase in email open rates by the end of Q2." This not only keeps you on track but also allows for timely adjustments if needed. Aligning marketing goals with business objectives ensures that every marketing effort supports the overall strategy. Whether it's increasing brand awareness, generating qualified leads, enhancing customer engagement, or boosting sales and revenue, your marketing goals should contribute to these broader objectives. For instance, if your business objective is to expand into a new market, your marketing goal could be to "increase brand awareness in the new market by 30% in six months" through targeted campaigns.

Using data to set goals is a game-changer. Analyzing past performance helps you understand what worked and what didn't. Use this data to set informed and realistic goals. Evaluating your business alongside competitors can yield valuable insights. Identify trends and opportunities by studying market data and consumer behavior. For instance, if data shows that video content drives more engagement in your industry, you might set a goal to "increase video content production by 50% in the next quarter." Leveraging data ensures your goals are grounded in reality and aligned with current market conditions.

***

Let's consider a case study to illustrate successful goal setting.

> A mid-sized e-commerce business wanted to boost its holiday sales. They set a SMART goal to "increase holiday sales by 25% compared to the previous year." They used data from past holiday seasons to identify peak shopping days and customer preferences. Their strategy included targeted email campaigns, social media promotions, and limited-time discounts. The results were impressive. They achieved a 30% increase in holiday sales, exceeding their goal.

The key takeaway is a clear, data-driven goals combined with well-planned strategies lead to success.

***

Identifying and Understanding Your Target Audience

Understanding who your audience is forms the basis of a winning marketing strategy. Imagine trying to sell ice cream in the middle of winter to people who are lactose intolerant. Without knowing who you're talking to, your efforts can easily miss the mark. Conducting audience research is your first step. Surveys and questionnaires are straightforward methods to gather information directly from your customers. You can ask about their preferences, habits, and pain points. Social media listening, on the other hand, involves monitoring what people are saying online about your brand and industry. This can offer real-time insights into consumer sentiment and trends.

Customer interviews provide a deeper understanding. Unlike surveys, interviews allow for open-ended questions that can uncover insights you might not have considered. These can be conducted in person, over the phone, or via video calls. Analyzing website analytics is another powerful tool. Tools like Google Analytics can show you where your traffic is coming from, what pages are most popular, and how long visitors stay. This data helps you understand what interests your audience and where you might need to improve.

Creating buyer personas brings your target audience to life. These personas are fictional characters that represent different segments of your audience. Start with demographic information such as age, gender, income, and education. Add psychographic details, which include interests, values, and pain points. For example, a buyer persona for a fitness brand might be "Sarah, a 30-year-old working professional who values health and wellness but struggles to find time for the gym." Behavioral insights round out the persona, detailing buying habits and online behavior. Knowing that Sarah prefers online shopping and follows fitness influencers can help tailor your marketing messages to her.

Segmenting your audience allows for more targeted marketing. Demographic segmentation divides your audience by age, gender, income, or education level. Geographic segmentation focuses on location, which is crucial for local businesses. Psychographic segmentation goes deeper, considering lifestyle, values, and personality traits. Behavioral segmentation looks at past behaviors, such as purchase history or website interactions. Each type of segmentation helps you create more personalized and effective marketing messages. For instance, a travel agency might use geographic segmentation to target beach vacation ads to people living in colder climates.

Utilizing audience insights involves more than just gathering data; it's about applying it effectively. Personalizing marketing messages is a key step. Use the information from your buyer personas to craft messages that resonate with different segments. Identifying the most effective marketing channels is equally important. If your audience spends most of their time on Instagram, focus your efforts there rather than spreading yourself thin across multiple platforms. Enhancing customer experience should always be a priority. Use audience insights to improve your website navigation, customer service, and overall user experience. Customers are more inclined to engage and convert when they feel understood and valued.

Understanding your target audience is an ongoing process, not a one-time task. It requires continual updates and adjustments to stay relevant. The better you know your audience, the more effective your marketing efforts will be. Use surveys, social media listening, customer interviews, and website analytics to keep your finger on the pulse. Create in-depth buyer personas to steer your strategic decisions. Segment your audience to deliver tailored messages. And always use these insights to enhance the customer experience. This comprehensive approach will ensure your marketing efforts are well-targeted and effective.

Choosing the Right Digital Marketing Channels

Navigating the digital marketing landscape means making smart choices about where to focus your efforts. Different channels offer various advantages and drawbacks, and understanding these will help you select the best fit for your business. Social media platforms like Facebook, Instagram, and LinkedIn are powerful tools for reaching diverse audiences. Facebook is great for community building and targeted ads, while Instagram excels in visual storytelling. LinkedIn, on the other hand, is ideal for business-to-business (B2B) marketing and professional networking. But, each comes with its own set of challenges, such as the need for consistent content and the ever-changing algorithms that can impact your reach.

Search engines such as Google and Bing are crucial for driving traffic through both organic and paid search methods. With Google dominating the search engine market, it is the primary choice for PPC campaigns and SEO strategies. Bing, while less popular, can offer cheaper PPC opportunities and less competition for keywords. Email marketing remains reliable in digital strategies, boasting one of the highest ROI among marketing channels. It's perfect for nurturing leads, engaging customers, and driving direct sales. Content marketing platforms like blogs and YouTube enable you to provide value through informative or entertaining content. Blogs can boost your SEO, while YouTube offers a massive audience for video content, which is increasingly popular.

Selecting the right channels involves aligning them with your audience and marketing goals. Audience preferences and behaviors are critical; if your target demographic spends most of their time on Instagram, it makes sense to focus there. Likewise, if your goal is lead generation, LinkedIn might be your best bet due to its professional user base. Understanding each channel's effectiveness for specific goals is pivotal. For instance, social media platforms are excellent for brand awareness and engagement, but search engines might be better for direct conversions. Tailoring your strategy to match these strengths will maximize your impact.

A multi-channel approach is often the most effective, as it allows you to reach your audience through various touchpoints. Cross-promotion strategies can help integrate your efforts across different platforms. For example, a blog post can be shared on social media, included in an email newsletter, and even turned into a video. Consistent messaging across channels ensures your brand stays recognizable and trustworthy. Tracking and measuring performance across these channels is vital. Tools like Google Analytics and social media insights can help you monitor your efforts and adjust as needed. Keeping tabs on your metrics will show you what's working and where you might need to pivot.

***

Consider a real-world example.

> A mid-sized retail business wanted to boost both online and in-store sales. They decided to focus on Facebook and Instagram for social media marketing, Google Ads for paid search, and an email newsletter to keep customers engaged. They used Facebook and Instagram to showcase new products and run targeted ads, driving traffic to their website. Google Ads helped capture high-intent searches, bringing in ready-to-buy customers. Their email newsletter kept the audience informed about sales and events. The result was a significant increase in both online traffic and in-store visits, proving the power of a well-integrated multi-channel strategy.

***

Differentiating Organic vs. Paid Search

Let's talk about organic search first. Organic search refers to the unpaid search results that appear on search engines like Google and Bing. These results are determined by the search engine's algorithms, which consider factors like relevance, quality, and user experience. Organic search relies heavily on SEO strategies, which can be divided into on-page and off-page techniques. On-page SEO involves optimizing elements on your website, such as content, meta tags, and internal links. Off-page SEO, meanwhile, focuses on building backlinks from other reputable sites to increase your site's authority. One of the main benefits of organic search is its cost-effectiveness. Unlike paid ads, you don't have to pay for clicks, making it a budget-friendly option for long-term growth. Moreover, organic search helps build trust and credibility. Users often trust organic results more than ads because they know these sites have earned their spot through quality and relevance.

Now, let's shift to paid search. Paid search, also known as PPC advertising, involves paying for your ads to appear on search engine results pages. Google Ads and Bing Ads are popular platforms for running PPC campaigns. When you run a PPC campaign, you bid on keywords relevant to your business. Your ad appears when someone searches for those keywords, and you pay each time someone clicks on your ad. One of the biggest advantages of paid search is the immediacy of results. While SEO takes time to build, PPC can drive traffic to your site almost instantly. It's a great way to generate leads and sales quickly. Paid search also offers targeted reach. You can customize your ads to reach specific locations, demographics, and even times of day, ensuring your marketing dollars are spent efficiently.

Comparing organic and paid search reveals distinct differences. Cost is a significant factor. Organic search is cost-effective, requiring an investment of time and effort but not direct payment for clicks. Paid search, on the other hand, involves ongoing costs that can add up quickly. However, while organic search provides long-term benefits, it takes time and consistent effort to see results. Paid search offers immediate visibility but requires continuous spending to maintain that visibility. Expertise and effort levels also vary. SEO demands a deep understanding of algorithms, keyword research, and content creation. PPC involves managing bids, ad copy, and budgeting, often requiring specialized knowledge for optimal results.

Integrating both organic and paid search strategies can yield the best results. Start by balancing your budget and resources. Allocate funds for PPC to generate immediate traffic while investing in SEO for sustainable growth. Use data from your paid campaigns to inform your organic strategies. For example, identify high-performing keywords in your PPC campaigns and target them in your SEO efforts. This synergy ensures you're maximizing your reach and effectiveness across both channels. By leveraging the strengths of both approaches, you can create a robust digital marketing strategy that drives both immediate and long-term success.

Creating a Content Calendar for Consistency

A content calendar is your secret weapon for staying organized and consistent in your content marketing efforts. Imagine the chaos of trying to remember what to post and when, especially when juggling multiple platforms and types of content. A content calendar solves this by ensuring regular content publication, planning around key dates and events, and coordinating efforts across your team. By mapping out your content in advance, you avoid the last-minute scramble and maintain a steady flow of engaging material that keeps your audience hooked. It's like having a well-organized pantry, where you know exactly what's in stock and what needs to be replenished.

Creating a content calendar involves several steps. Start by identifying content themes and topics that align with your marketing goals and audience interests. Think about the problems your audience faces and how your content can provide solutions. Once you have your themes, schedule content publication dates. This helps you stay consistent and ensures you're posting regularly. Assign content creation responsibilities to team members to spread the workload evenly. This not only keeps everyone accountable but also brings diverse perspectives to your content. Incorporate content repurposing strategies to get the most mileage out of your work. For example, a blog post can be turned into a video, an infographic, and several social media posts, maximizing its reach.

Managing a content calendar can be made easier with the right tools. Trello is a popular choice for its visual boards and easy drag-and-drop interface. It allows you to create cards for each piece of content and move them through different stages of creation. Asana is another great tool, offering task management features that help keep your team on track. Google Sheets is a simple yet effective option, especially if you're looking for a customizable solution. You can create a spreadsheet with columns for dates, topics, authors, and publication status. CoSchedule is a more advanced tool that integrates with various platforms, offering features like automated publishing and detailed analytics.

Best practices for content planning revolve around ensuring quality and relevance. Align your content with your audience's needs and interests by regularly reviewing feedback and engagement metrics. This helps you understand what resonates and adjust your strategy accordingly. Incorporate diverse content formats to keep things interesting. Mix up your blogs with videos, infographics, and podcasts to cater to different preferences. Consistently reviewing and refreshing your content calendar is key to staying on track. The digital landscape is dynamic, and your content plan should be flexible enough to adapt to changes. Schedule regular check-ins to assess what's working, what's not, and make necessary adjustments. This ongoing evaluation ensures your content remains fresh, relevant, and effective in achieving your marketing goals.

Budgeting for Your Digital Marketing Efforts

Having a clear marketing budget is crucial for effective digital marketing. It ensures you allocate resources efficiently, measure ROI, and avoid overspending. Without a budget, it's easy to pour money into ineffective strategies, leaving you with little to show for your efforts. A well-planned budget helps you focus on what matters most, aligning your spending with your goals. For instance, if your main objective is to boost brand awareness, you might allocate more funds to social media advertising and content creation. On the other hand, if driving sales is your priority, investing in PPC campaigns and email marketing could be more effective.

Creating a marketing budget involves several steps. Start by assessing your current financial situation. Look at your overall revenue and determine how much you can realistically allocate to marketing. Next, estimate the costs for different channels and tactics. Research industry benchmarks and gather quotes from service providers to get a clear picture of expenses. Prioritize your spending based on your goals and past performance. If social media ads have previously driven significant traffic, allocate more funds there. Allow for flexibility and unexpected expenses. Marketing landscapes change, and having a buffer can help you adapt without derailing your entire strategy.

Tracking and adjusting your budget are ongoing tasks. Regular budget reviews help you stay on track and make informed decisions. Use budget tracking tools like Quick-Books or Excel to monitor your spending. These tools can provide insights into where your money is going and whether it's yielding the expected ROI. Adjust your budget based on campaign performance. If a particular strategy is underperforming, reallocate funds to more effective tactics. This flexibility ensures you maximize your ROI and avoid wasting resources. For example, if your email marketing campaign is outperforming your social media ads, consider shifting more budget towards email to capitalize on its success.

Let's consider a case study to illustrate effective marketing budget management.

A small e-commerce business wanted to increase its online sales. They started with a modest budget and allocated funds across different channels: SEO, PPC, social media, and email marketing. They prioritized spending based on past performance, dedicating the most budget to PPC and social media ads, which had previously shown strong results. They also set aside a small portion for unexpected expenses. Throughout the campaign, they used QuickBooks to track spending and regularly reviewed their budget. When they noticed that their email marketing was driving higher conversions, they reallocated some funds from social media ads to email campaigns. The result was 25% increase in online sales, demonstrating the power of strategic budget management.

The key takeaway here is the importance of flexibility and continuous monitoring to ensure you're getting the best return on your investment.

In summary, budgeting for your digital marketing efforts is not just about setting aside money; it's about making informed decisions that align with your business goals. A well-planned budget helps you allocate resources efficiently, measure ROI, and stay flexible. By regularly tracking and adjusting your budget, you can maximize your marketing effectiveness and achieve your business objectives. This sets the stage for the next chapter, where we'll dive into mastering search engine optimization for long-term success.

Chapter Three

Search Engine Optimization Mastery

Navigating the world of SEO can feel like trying to solve a puzzle without all the pieces. Just when you think you have it figured out, Google changes its algorithm, and you're back to square one. But here's the deal: understanding and optimizing for SEO isn't just about keeping up with Google's whims. It's about creating a website that not only ranks well but also provides a fantastic user experience. Let's dive into some of the best practices for SEO that will keep you ahead of the curve now and beyond.

SEO Best Practices for Now and Beyond

One of the hottest trends you can't ignore is voice search optimization. With the rise of smart speakers and virtual assistants like Alexa and Siri, more people are using voice commands to search online. This changes how keywords are used. Instead of typing "best pizza near me," users might ask, "Where can I find the best pizza nearby?" This means your content needs to be optimized for natural language and long-tail keywords. Anticipate the questions your customers might ask and craft content that provides clear answers.

Another trend is mobile-first indexing. Google now primarily uses the mobile version of your site for indexing and ranking. If your site isn't mobile-friendly, you're missing out. Make sure your website is built to be responsive, adjusting to fit any screen size. Check that buttons and links are easily clickable, and text is readable without zooming. Mobile users expect a seamless experience, and Google rewards sites that deliver it.

Core Web Vitals are another critical factor. These metrics measure the user experience based on page load speed, interactivity, and visual stability. A fast-loading, stable page keeps users happy, and Google takes notice. Tools like Google's PageSpeed Insights can help you identify areas for improvement. Aim for a first input delay of less than 100 milliseconds and a cumulative layout shift of under 0.1 to ensure a smooth user experience.

AI and machine learning are playing an increasingly significant role in shaping search algorithms. Google's AI, known as RankBrain, helps interpret complex queries and deliver more relevant results. This means your content needs to be more relevant and engaging than ever. Focus on creating high-quality content that answers users' questions and keeps them on your site longer. The longer users stay, the more signals Google receives that your content is valuable.

User experience (UX) is crucial for SEO rankings. Google's algorithms increasingly favor sites that offer a great UX. Page load speed significantly impacts UX. A slow site can frustrate users, leading to higher bounce rates. Compress images, use browser caching, and minimize HTTP requests to speed up your site. Mobile responsiveness ensures that users on smartphones and tablets have a seamless experience. Design your site to be intuitive and easy to navigate, with clear calls to action. User-friendly navigation keeps visitors on your site longer, reducing bounce rates and improving your rankings.

Google's E-A-T guidelines, Expertise, Authoritativeness, Trustworthiness, are essential for SEO. Expertise involves creating content that demonstrates a deep understanding of the topic. Establish author credentials by showcasing their experience and qualifications. Authoritativeness is built through backlinks from reputable sites and mentions from industry experts. Trustworthiness is about creating a secure and reliable site. Use secure sockets layer (SSL) certificates to ensure your site is secure, and encourage user reviews to build trust with visitors.

Practical Optimization Tips

To optimize your website, start by updating and repurposing old content. Freshness matters to Google, so regularly update your content to keep it relevant. Implement structured data and schema markup to enhance search engines' understanding of your content. This can improve your chances of appearing in rich snippets, which can boost your click-through rates. Optimize your images and videos by using descriptive file names, adding alternative (alt) text, and compressing them to improve page load speed.

By focusing on these SEO best practices, you'll be well-equipped to navigate the ever-changing landscape of search engine optimization.

Keyword Research and Selection

Keyword research forms the foundation of successful SEO efforts. Imagine trying to sell your product in a crowded market without knowing what your customers are looking for. Without keyword research, you're essentially doing just that. It helps you understand user intent, which is crucial. Are people looking for information, or are they ready to buy? Understanding this guides you in creating content that meets their needs. Identifying high-traffic keywords is another benefit. These are the terms people are frequently searching for. But it's not just about traffic; you also need to balance competition and search volume. High-traffic keywords are great, but if the competition is fierce, it can be tough to rank. Balancing these factors ensures you target keywords that not only attract visitors but also give you a fighting chance to rank.

Let's break down the keyword research process. Start by brainstorming seed keywords. These are broad terms related to your business. For example, if you run a fitness studio, seed keywords might include "fitness classes," "yoga," and "personal training." Once you have a list, it's time to dive deeper using keyword research tools. Google Keyword Planner is an excellent tool to begin your keyword research. It shows you search volumes and suggests related keywords. Ahrefs and SEMrush offer more advanced features, including keyword difficulty scores. These scores help you gauge how hard it will be to rank for a particular keyword. Analyzing keyword difficulty and search volume ensures you target the right mix of low-competition and high-traffic keywords, setting you up for success.

There are several tools you can use for keyword research. Google Keyword Planner is a free tool that provides valuable insights into search volumes and keyword trends. SEMrush is an all-in-one platform that not only helps with keyword research but also offers competitor analysis. It's great for finding out which keywords your competitors rank for. Ahrefs is another comprehensive tool that excels in backlink analysis and keyword research. It offers a keyword difficulty score, which is useful for prioritizing your efforts. Ubersuggest, created by Neil Patel, is a tool that provides keyword suggestions, competition data, and search volume and is user-friendly. Each tool has its strengths, and using a combination can give you a well-rounded view of your keyword landscape.

Understanding the difference between long-tail and short-tail keywords is crucial. Short-tail keywords are broad terms like "shoes" or "laptops." They have significant search volumes but face strong competition. Long-tail keywords, on the other hand, are more specific phrases like "best budget running shoes for women." They have lower search volumes but are less competitive and often result in higher conversion rates. Targeting long-tail keywords is beneficial for several reasons. They attract more targeted traffic, meaning visitors are more likely to convert. For example, someone searching for "best budget running shoes for women" is probably ready to make a purchase. This specificity reduces competition, making it easier to rank higher in search results.

Keyword mapping is a strategic process that ensures your keywords are effectively distributed across your website. Start by creating a keyword map, which is a document outlining which keywords will be targeted on which pages. Assign both primary and secondary keywords to each page for optimal SEO performance. The primary keyword should be the main focus, while secondary keywords provide additional context. Ensuring keyword relevance to content is vital. Each page should be optimized for its assigned keywords without keyword stuffing. This approach not only enhances SEO but also boosts user experience by delivering relevant content. Strategically mapping keywords helps prevent keyword cannibalization, where multiple pages target the same keyword, weakening your overall SEO impact.

On-Page SEO: Optimizing Individual Web Pages

A key starting point for on-page SEO is optimizing your title tags and meta descriptions. These elements are your first impression in search results, so they need to be spot-on. Title tags should include your primary keywords and stay within the 50-60 character limit to avoid being cut off in search results. Think of them as the headline of an article, they need to be compelling and to the point. Meta descriptions, although not a direct ranking factor, are vital for enhancing your click-through rate (CTR). Aim for around 150-160 characters and make sure it's persuasive. Include a call-to-action like "Learn more" or "Get started" to entice users to click.

Header tags and content structure are next on the list. Header tags (H1, H2, H3, etc.) help organize your content, making it easier for both users and search engines to understand. The H1 tag should be used for the main heading of your page, and it should include your primary keyword. H2 and H3 tags are for subheadings and should also be keyword-rich. Proper use of header tags enhances the readability of your content, which improves user experience and, in turn, boosts your SEO. A well-structured page not only keeps readers engaged but also signals to search engines that your content is well-organized and valuable.

Internal linking strategies are often overlooked but are incredibly effective. Internal links distribute link equity across your site and help users navigate more easily. When writing a blog post, link to related posts to keep readers on your site longer. Use anchor text that includes relevant keywords rather than generic terms like "click here." This not only improves the user experience but also helps search engines understand the context of the linked pages. A logical internal linking structure makes it easier for search engines to crawl your site, improving your overall SEO performance.

Image optimization is an essential element of on-page SEO. Large image files can slow down your page loading speed, which harms both user experience and SEO performance. Use descriptive file names for your images, incorporating keywords where relevant. Adding alt text to images not only makes your site more accessible but also provides another opportunity to include keywords. Compress images using tools like TinyPNG to reduce file size without sacrificing quality, ensuring faster loading times. Faster pages keep users happy and improve your search engine rankings.

By focusing on these aspects of on-page SEO, you can significantly enhance your website's performance and user experience. Optimizing title tags and meta descriptions, using header tags effectively, implementing a solid internal linking strategy, and optimizing images are all steps that can lead to better search engine rankings and a more engaging site for your visitors.

Off-Page SEO: Building Authority and Trust

Building high-quality backlinks is like getting endorsements from respected figures in your industry. These backlinks signal to search engines that your site is credible and worth ranking higher. But not all backlinks are created equal. Aim to earn links from authoritative sites, avoiding low-quality or spammy backlinks that can do more harm than good. Guest posting on reputable blogs is a tried-and-true method. Reach out to sites relevant to your niche and offer to write valuable content in exchange for a backlink. This not only boosts your SEO but also positions you as an expert in your field. Additionally, create shareable content such as infographics and research reports. These assets naturally attract backlinks because they provide value that others want to share.

There are several strategies you can use to build high-quality backlinks. Guest blogging remains a powerful tool. By contributing high-quality articles to reputable sites, you gain exposure and valuable links. Another effective method is creating linkable content assets. Infographics, comprehensive research reports, and in-depth guides are often cited by other websites, earning you backlinks. Outreach and relationship building are also crucial. Connect with influencers and bloggers in your industry. Building these relationships can lead to natural backlink opportunities, whether through collaborations, mentions, or guest posts.

Social media engagement indirectly benefits SEO by driving traffic and generating backlinks. When you share your content on social media, you increase its visibility. More people see it, share it, and potentially link to it from their websites. This boosts your brand awareness and drives referral traffic. Engaging with influencers and participating in relevant online communities can amplify these effects. For instance, sharing blog posts and articles on platforms like Twitter and LinkedIn can lead to more shares and backlinks. Engaging with influencers by commenting on their posts and sharing their content can also build relationships that result in backlink opportunities.

Managing your online reputation is a key factor in off-page SEO. Encourage positive reviews from satisfied customers. These reviews not only build trust with potential customers but also contribute to your online authority. Addressing negative feedback promptly and professionally shows that you care about your customers and are committed to resolving issues. Building brand authority involves consistently delivering high-quality products or services and engaging positively with your audience. A positive online presence, reflected in reviews, social media interactions, and customer testimonials, enhances your credibility and trustworthiness.

Content marketing is a highly effective strategy for building backlinks and improving off-page SEO. Focus on creating valuable, shareable content that others want to link to. Infographics and visual content are particularly powerful because they are easily digestible and visually appealing. Promote your content through outreach and guest blogging. Reach out to sites that might find your content valuable and offer to let them share it. This not only earns you backlinks but also expands your reach to new audiences.

Building high-quality backlinks, engaging on social media, managing your online reputation, and leveraging content marketing are all crucial components of off-page SEO. By focusing on these strategies, you can build authority and trust, significantly boosting your search engine rankings.

Technical SEO: Enhancing Website Performance

Improving site speed is crucial for both SEO and user experience. Imagine visiting a website that takes forever to load; you'd probably leave before it even finishes. Google's algorithms take page load speed into account, meaning a slow site can hurt your rankings. Tools like Google PageSpeed Insights are invaluable for diagnosing speed issues. They break down elements slowing your site and offer suggestions for improvement. Minimizing HTTP requests is one effective strategy. Each file on your page, images, scripts, stylesheets, requires a separate request. Reducing these can significantly speed up your site. Enabling browser caching allows returning visitors to load your pages faster by storing some elements of your site in their browser. Compressing files, especially images and videos, can also make a big difference. Smaller files load quicker, improving the overall speed of your site.

Mobile optimization is non-negotiable in the age of mobile-first indexing. Google primarily uses the mobile version of a site for indexing and ranking. If your site isn't optimized for mobile, you're at a disadvantage. Responsive design principles ensure your site adapts to various screen sizes, providing a seamless experience whether users are on a phone, tablet, or desktop. Fast load times are essential on mobile devices, where users often have slower internet connections. Using Google's Mobile-Friendly Test, you can check how easily a visitor can use your page on a mobile device. This tool highlights issues and provides recommendations for making your site more mobile-friendly.

XML sitemaps and robots.txt files guide search engines in crawling and indexing your site effectively. An XML sitemap is like a roadmap for search engines, listing all your site's pages. Creating and submitting an XML sitemap helps search engines find and index your content faster. Use tools like Google Search Console to submit your sitemap and monitor its status. The robots.txt file tells search engines which parts of your site to crawl and which to ignore. Configuring robots.txt correctly ensures search engines focus on your most important pages without getting bogged down by irrelevant content. Regularly check your Search Console to ensure your sitemap and robots.txt are functioning as intended.

Fixing crawl errors is essential for maintaining a healthy site. Crawl errors occur when search engines encounter issues accessing your pages. These errors can prevent important content from being indexed, hurting your SEO. Google Search Console is an excellent tool for identifying crawl errors. It provides a list of issues like 404 errors (pages not found) and broken links. Fixing these errors should be a priority. Correct 404 errors by redirecting them to relevant pages using 301 redirects. Ensure all internal and external links are functional to maintain a smooth user experience. Properly managing crawl errors keeps search engines happy and ensures your content gets the visibility it deserves.

Local SEO for Small Businesses

Local SEO is vital for small businesses aiming to attract local customers. Picture this: Someone in your town searches for a service you offer. If your business doesn't appear in the local search results, you've missed out on a potential customer. Local search behavior trends show that people increasingly rely on search engines to find local businesses. Think about it; how often do you use your phone to look up the nearest coffee shop or plumber? Appearing in local search results not only drives foot traffic but also builds your local brand presence. A strong local SEO strategy ensures you're visible when it matters most.

Setting up Google My Business (GMB) is a cornerstone of local SEO. Start by creating a GMB account. It's straightforward: go to the Google My Business website and sign up using your Google account. Once you're in, add accurate business information. This includes your business name, address, phone number, and hours of operation. Make sure everything is correct; inconsistencies can confuse potential customers and search engines alike. Next, encourage customer reviews. Positive reviews boost your credibility and improve your rankings. Ask satisfied customers to leave a review and respond to them, thanking them for their feedback. This interaction not only builds trust but also shows Google that your business is active and engaged.

Local citations and directories are vital for local SEO, as they provide online mentions of your business's name, address, and phone number (NAP). Consistency is key here. Ensure your NAP information is identical across all platforms, from Yelp to the Yellow Pages. Inconsistent information can hurt your rankings and confuse customers. Use tools like Moz Local to manage your citations. These tools help you find and correct inconsistencies, ensuring your business information is accurate everywhere it appears. Listing your business in local directories not only improves your visibility but also builds backlinks, further boosting your SEO.

Optimizing for local keywords is another essential step. Local keywords include your location and the services you offer. Conduct local keyword research to find terms your potential customers are using. Tools like Google Keyword Planner can help identify these keywords. Once you have a list, integrate them into your website content. Add location-based keywords to your title tags and meta descriptions. For example, if you're a bakery in Austin, use phrases like "best bakery in Austin" or "Austin custom cakes."

Creating local content, such as blog posts about local events or community involvement, can also help. This not only attracts local traffic but also shows you're an active part of the community.

In summary, local SEO is a powerful tool for small businesses looking to attract local customers. By setting up and optimizing your Google My Business profile, ensuring consistency across local citations, and targeting local keywords, you can significantly improve your visibility in local search results. This not only drives more foot traffic to your business but also helps you build a strong local brand presence. Keep these strategies in mind as you develop your SEO plan, and you'll be well on your way to local success.

Chapter Four

Social Media Marketing Excellence

I magine having a megaphone that lets you speak directly to millions of potential customers. That's the power of social media marketing. But with great power comes great responsibility, or in this case, the need for a smart strategy. Social media can be a game-changer for your business. However, choosing the right platforms and understanding where your audience spends their time is crucial. Let's break it down, so you can make informed decisions and maximize your social media efforts.

Choosing the Right Social Media Platforms

First off, let's talk about understanding audience preferences. Knowing where your target audience spends their time online is the first step in choosing the right platforms. Analyzing demographic data helps you identify which platforms are most popular among your target age groups, genders, and interests. For instance, if your target audience is primarily teenagers, Instagram and TikTok are your go-to platforms. On the other hand, LinkedIn is a goldmine for professionals and B2B marketing.

Conducting surveys can offer valuable insights into platform preferences. Ask your existing customers which social media platforms they use the most. This direct feedback can guide your strategy and help you focus your efforts on the platforms that matter. Social media analytics are another powerful tool. Facebook Insights, Instagram Analytics, and Twitter (now X) Analytics can show you where your audience is most engaged. These insights help you see which posts are performing well and where your audience is spending their time, providing a clearer picture of where to invest your resources.

Each social media platform has its unique features and strengths, making them suited for different objectives. Facebook is fantastic for community building and advertising. With nearly three billion active users monthly, it offers a diverse demographic reach and advanced targeting options for ads. Facebook Pages and Groups can enhance brand visibility and engagement, while Messenger can serve as a robust customer service tool. Instagram, on the other hand, is a visual-centric platform ideal for storytelling. Its features like Stories, Videos (short and long), and Shopping make it perfect for businesses looking to build a strong brand identity and drive e-commerce sales. Collaborating with influencers and leveraging user-generated content can further amplify your reach.

LinkedIn stands out for professional networking and B2B marketing. It's the platform where you can demonstrate leadership and industry expertise. Optimizing your personal and company profiles, engaging in discussions, and sharing valuable content can help you build a professional network. LinkedIn's targeted advertising options are particularly effective for B2B businesses. X (formerly known as Twitter) excels in real-time updates and customer service. It's a platform where you can engage in conversations, respond to customer queries, and share timely updates. The fast-paced nature of X makes it a powerful tool for customer engagement and brand awareness.

Aligning social media platforms with your business goals is essential for maximizing your efforts. If your objective is brand awareness, platforms like Instagram and Facebook are ideal due to their vast user base and visual content capabilities. For lead generation, LinkedIn and X offer excellent opportunities. LinkedIn's professional network is perfect for B2B marketing, while X's real-time engagement can drive traffic and leads. When it comes to customer engagement, Facebook Groups and Instagram Stories are invaluable. They allow for direct interaction with your audience, fostering a sense of community and loyalty.

***

Let's look at a case study to illustrate successful platform selection.

> H&M, a popular fashion brand, leveraged a mix of virtual content creators and engaging campaign videos on Instagram. The brand launched a series of Instagram ads to promote their *Innovation Metaverse Design Story* collection. This innovative approach captured the imagination of their target audience, leading to a dramatic *11-fold increase in ad recall*. Even more impressively, the strategy slashed the cost per person recalling the ad by *91%*, showcasing the power of combining cutting-edge content with strategic ad placement. The campaign's success is a testament to how immersive storytelling and digital creativity can revolutionize engagement and drive impactful results.

***

Understanding your audience, evaluating platform features, and aligning them with your business goals are crucial steps in choosing the right social media platforms. By focusing your efforts where they matter most, you can maximize your reach, engagement, and ultimately, your business success.

Creating Engaging Social Media Content

Creating engaging social media content isn't just about posting pretty pictures or catchy phrases. It's about crafting content that resonates with your audience and keeps them coming back for more. Different types of content serve different purposes, and understanding these can help you make the most of your social media efforts. Images and infographics, for example, are visual and easily digestible. They can convey complex information quickly and are highly shareable. A well-designed infographic on industry trends or a beautiful image of your product can catch the eye and be shared widely, increasing your reach.

Videos and live streams are another powerful tool. They allow you to connect with your audience on a more personal level. A behind-the-scenes video of your team at work, a product demonstration, or a live Q&A session can humanize your brand and build trust. Live streams, in particular, offer real-time interaction, making your audience feel involved and valued. Stories and ephemeral content, like those on Instagram and Facebook, create a sense of urgency. They disappear after 24 hours, encouraging your audience to engage quickly. This format is perfect for limited-time offers, behind-the-scenes glimpses, or daily updates.

Storytelling is an effective tool for crafting engaging content. Every brand has its own story, and by sharing yours, you can build a meaningful emotional connection with your audience. Craft a brand narrative that highlights your values, mission, and the journey you've taken to get where you are. Customer success stories are another great way to use storytelling. Share testimonials and case studies that showcase how your product or service has made a difference in your customers' lives. Behind-the-scenes content can also be engaging. Show your team at work, share the process of creating a product, or give a glimpse into your company culture. This transparency builds trust and makes your brand more relatable.

Interactive content such as quizzes and polls can greatly enhance audience engagement. People love sharing their opinions and testing their knowledge. A poll about a new product feature or a fun quiz related to your industry can spark conversation and keep your audience engaged. This type of content not only entertains, but also offers valuable insights into your audience's preferences and opinions.

Creating visually appealing content is essential for capturing attention in the fast-paced world of social media. Use high-quality images and videos that are consistent with your brand's visual identity. Consistent branding is crucial; ensure your colors, fonts, and logos are uniform across all your content. This not only makes your posts recognizable but also reinforces your brand identity. Incorporating user-generated content can also enhance your visuals. Encourage your customers to share photos of themselves using your product and repost these images on your account. This not only provides you with fresh content but also builds a sense of community and trust.

Planning your content in advance is crucial for maintaining consistency. Using a content calendar as we previously discussed helps you organize what to post and when, ensuring you don't run out of ideas or miss important dates. Balance is key in your content calendar. Mix promotional content with value-driven posts that educate, entertain, or inspire your audience. For every post promoting your product, include several that provide value without asking for anything in return. This builds trust and keeps your audience engaged.

Building and Nurturing Your Online Community

Building an engaged online community is like cultivating a thriving garden. It requires the right strategies, consistent attention, and a touch of creativity. One effective way to build a community is by creating and managing Facebook groups. These groups offer a space where your audience can connect, share experiences, and discuss topics related to your brand. As the group admin, you can foster discussions, share exclusive content, and provide support, creating a sense of belonging among members. Hosting live Q&A sessions is another fantastic strategy. These sessions allow you to interact with your audience in real-time, answer their questions, and build a personal connection. It's like having a casual chat over coffee, making your brand more relatable and trustworthy. Encouraging user-generated content is also powerful. When customers share their own experiences with your product, it not only provides social proof but also engages other users. Running social media contests and giveaways can boost engagement and attract new followers. People love the chance to win something, and these contests can create a buzz around your brand.

Engaging with your audience is crucial for building a loyal community. It's not enough to just post content; you need to actively interact with your followers. Responding to comments and messages promptly shows that you value their input and are there to help. It's like having a conversation; no one likes being ignored. Asking questions can encourage interaction and make your audience feel involved. For example, if you're a beauty brand, ask your followers about their favorite skincare routines. Sharing and celebrating user content is another way to engage. Reposting customer photos or highlighting their stories makes them feel appreciated and encourages others to share as well. Hosting regular live sessions and webinars can deepen your connection with your audience. These events provide value, whether it's through educational content, product updates, or just a fun chat, and they show that you're invested in your community.

Creating a welcoming and supportive community culture is essential for long-term engagement. Setting clear community guidelines helps maintain a positive environment. These guidelines should outline acceptable behavior, the types of content allowed, and how conflicts are handled. Think of them as the ground rules for a friendly neighborhood. Moderating discussions effectively is also important. Keep an eye on conversations to ensure they stay respectful and on-topic. Recognizing and rewarding active members can boost morale and encourage continued participation. A simple shoutout or a small reward for contributions can go a long way in making members feel valued.

Measuring community engagement helps you understand what's working and where you can improve. Engagement rate, which includes likes, comments, and shares, is a key metric. It shows how actively your audience is interacting with your content. Growth in followers and group members is another indicator of a thriving community. Sentiment analysis tools can provide insights into how your community feels about your brand. These tools analyze comments and messages to gauge the overall sentiment, whether it's positive, negative, or neutral. Tracking hashtag performance can also offer valuable insights. Hashtags help organize content and increase its visibility, making it easier for users to find. By analyzing which hashtags are driving engagement, you can refine your strategy to maximize reach.

By focusing on building and nurturing an engaged online community, you create a loyal base of followers who are invested in your brand. This not only boosts your reach and engagement but also fosters a sense of belonging and trust among your audience.

Social Media Advertising: Strategies and Best Practices

Social media advertising offers a dynamic way to reach your audience with precision and efficiency. Imagine being able to target your ads to specific demographics, interests, and behaviors. That's the magic of social media advertising. It provides unparalleled reach and targeting capabilities, allowing you to connect with potential customers who are most likely to be interested in your offerings. Compared to traditional advertising, social media ads are cost-effective. You can start with a modest budget and scale up as you see results.

Detailed performance metrics also set social media advertising apart. You can track every click, conversion, and engagement, allowing you to optimize your campaigns in real-time.

There are several types of social media ads available, each with its unique benefits. Facebook and Instagram ads offer a range of formats, including carousel ads, video ads, and stories. Carousel ads allow you to showcase multiple products or features within a single ad, making them great for e-commerce. Video ads can capture attention and convey your message in an engaging way. Stories, which are short-lived and full-screen, create a sense of urgency and are perfect for time-sensitive promotions. LinkedIn sponsored content is ideal for B2B marketing. It allows you to share valuable content, such as articles and case studies, directly in the LinkedIn feed, targeting professionals based on their industry, job title, and more. Twitter (now X) promoted tweets can amplify your reach, ensuring your tweets are seen by a broader audience. These ads are integrated seamlessly into the Twitter feed, making them less intrusive and more likely to engage users.

Creating effective ad campaigns involves several key steps. First, set clear objectives. What do you want to achieve? Is it brand awareness, lead generation, or sales? Clear goals steer your strategy and allow you to assess success accurately. Next, select the right ad format. If you're promoting a new product line, a carousel ad on Instagram might be ideal. For sharing industry insights, LinkedIn sponsored content could be more effective. Crafting compelling ad copy and visuals is invaluable. Your ad needs to grab attention and convey your message quickly. Use high-quality images or videos and write concise, persuasive copy. Targeting the right audience is essential. Social media platforms offer sophisticated targeting options, allowing you to reach people based on demographics, interests, and behaviors. Utilize these tools to ensure your ads are seen by those most likely to engage with them.

Budgeting and bidding strategies play a significant role in maximizing your ROI. Start by setting a daily or lifetime budget. A daily budget ensures you don't overspend in a single day, while a lifetime budget gives you more flexibility over a campaign's duration. Decide between CPC (Cost Per Click) and CPM (Cost Per Mille) bidding. CPC is ideal when you want to pay only for clicks, making it cost-effective for driving traffic. CPM, which charges per thousand impressions, is better for brand awareness campaigns. Monitoring and adjusting bids based on performance is crucial. Regularly review your campaign analytics and adjust your bids to ensure you're getting the best results for your budget.

Analyzing ad performance is essential for optimizing your campaigns. Use analytics tools like Facebook Ads Manager and Google Analytics to track key metrics such as conversion rates, click-through rates, and return on ad spend. These tools provide insights into what's working and what's not, allowing you to make data-driven decisions. For instance, if your video ads are outperforming carousel ads, you might allocate more budget to video. Regularly reviewing these metrics helps you refine your strategy, ensuring your ads remain effective and cost-efficient. Understanding these aspects of social media advertising will enable you to create campaigns that not only reach your target audience but also drive meaningful results.

Influencer Marketing: Building Authentic Partnerships

Selecting the right influencers is pivotal for any successful campaign. Start by researching influencer demographics and audience. An influencer might have a huge following, but if their audience doesn't align with your target market, it's a mismatch. Use tools like Social Blade or HypeAuditor to analyze their follower demographics, engagement rates, and growth patterns. Look for influencers who share similar values to your brand. If you're a sustainable fashion brand, an influencer who promotes eco-friendly lifestyles will resonate more with your audience. Engagement and authenticity are equally important. High engagement rates indicate an active, interested audience. Authenticity can be gauged through the influencer's content quality and how genuinely they interact with their followers. Avoid influencers with a high number of fake followers; these often result in low engagement and poor ROI.

Building genuine relationships with influencers takes time and effort but pays off in the long run. Start by personalizing your outreach messages. A generic email will likely end up in the trash. Mention specific posts of theirs you enjoyed or how you discovered them. This shows you've done your homework and are genuinely interested in a partnership. Offering value and incentives is another key strategy. What can you provide that benefits them? It could be monetary compensation, free products, or exclusive access to events. Collaborating on creative content ideas can also strengthen the relationship. Instead of dictating what you want, involve them in the creative process. Influencers know their audience best, and their input can make the campaign more authentic and engaging.

Planning and executing successful influencer campaigns require clear goals and KPIs. What do you want to achieve? Is it brand awareness, website traffic, or sales? Setting specific, measurable goals helps you track success and make necessary adjustments. Co-creating content with influencers allows for a more authentic representation of your brand. Whether it's a product review, an unboxing video, or a day-in-the-life post, let the influencer's personality shine through. Leveraging multiple platforms can broaden your reach. An Instagram post might drive immediate engagement, while a YouTube video provides more in-depth content. Combining different platforms maximizes your campaign's impact.

Measuring the success of influencer marketing efforts is crucial for understanding ROI. Start by monitoring engagement and reach. Use analytics tools to track likes, comments, shares, and overall reach of the posts. Evaluating ROI involves comparing the cost of the campaign against the revenue generated. This can be tracked through unique discount codes, affiliate links, or UTM parameters (snippets of test at the end of a URL, allowing you to track where engagement originated). Gathering feedback from both influencers and your audience provides valuable insights. Ask influencers for their thoughts on the campaign's effectiveness and areas for improvement. Similarly, engage with your audience to understand their perceptions and reactions. This feedback loop helps refine future campaigns for better results.

Measuring Social Media Success

Setting up social media analytics is like setting the foundation of a house. Without it, you won't know if your walls are straight or your roof is secure. Social media analytics tools are necessary for tracking your performance and understanding what works and what doesn't. Native analytics tools like Facebook Insights, Instagram Insights, and Twitter (X) Analytics provide a wealth of data. Facebook Insights, for instance, shows you how your posts are performing, who your audience is, and when they're most active. Instagram Insights offers similar metrics, focusing on engagement, reach, and follower demographics. Twitter Analytics provides data on tweet impressions, engagement rates, and follower growth.

Third-party tools can offer even more in-depth analysis. Hootsuite, for example, not only allows you to schedule posts but also provides comprehensive analytics across multiple platforms. Sprout Social is another excellent tool that offers advanced reporting and social listening features. These tools can help you track engagement, monitor brand mentions, and measure the effectiveness of your social media strategy. Setting up tracking and reporting is straightforward. Most tools allow you to customize your dashboards, choose which metrics to display, and set up automated reports. This means you can spend less time crunching numbers and more time optimizing your content.

Key metrics are your guide in the social media landscape. Engagement metrics, such as likes, comments, and shares, are important for understanding how your audience interacts with your content. High engagement shows that your content is connecting with your audience. Reach and impressions show you how many people see your posts. Reach indicates the unique users who see your content, while impressions count the total number of times your content is displayed. Follower growth measures how quickly your audience is expanding. A steady increase in followers is a good sign that your content is attracting new people. Conversion metrics, like click-through rate (CTR) and conversion rate, tell you how effective your social media efforts are at driving desired actions, such as website visits or purchases. Monitoring these metrics helps you gauge the success of your campaigns and identify areas for improvement.

. Analyzing and interpreting data is where the magic happens. It's not just about collecting data but understanding what it means. Look for trends and patterns in your metrics. For example, if you notice that posts with videos consistently get more engagement, it's a sign to create more video content. Compare performance across different platforms to see where you're getting the most bang for your buck. Maybe Instagram is driving more engagement, while LinkedIn is better for lead generation. Use this data to inform your future content and strategies. If a particular type of post performs well, replicate its elements in future posts. Similarly, if a platform isn't delivering results, consider reallocating resources to more effective channels.

Creating comprehensive reports is key for continuous improvement. Monthly social media reports help you keep track of your progress and make data-driven decisions. Include key metrics, insights, and actionable recommendations in your reports. Share these insights with your team to ensure everyone is aligned and informed. Implement changes based on data analysis. If your reports show that certain types of content or posting times yield better results, adjust your strategy accordingly. This iterative process ensures that your social media efforts are always evolving and improving.

By setting up robust analytics, monitoring key metrics, and continuously analyzing and reporting data, you can ensure your social media strategy is effective and aligned with your business goals. This sets the stage for the next chapter, where we'll get into the exciting world of email marketing strategies for success.

Chapter Five

Email Marketing Strategies for Success

E ver feel like your emails are just shouting into the void? It's a common struggle. You spend hours crafting the perfect message, only to see it go unopened or, worse, land in the spam folder. The key to avoiding this fate lies in building a high-quality email list. Let's dive into why this is important and how you can grow your list organically without resorting to shady tactics.

Building a High-Quality Email List

A high-quality email list is the backbone of successful email marketing. Imagine sending your carefully crafted messages to people who actually want to hear from you. Sounds ideal, right? Building your list through permission-based marketing is essential. Buying lists might seem like a quick fix, but it's fraught with problems. You'll end up with uninterested recipients who are likely to mark your emails as spam, damaging your sender reputation and lowering your engagement rates. Instead, focus on gaining permission. When people willingly sign up, they're already interested in what you have to offer. This builds trust and ensures higher engagement and conversion rates.

Trust is the foundation of any successful relationship, and email marketing is no different. When subscribers sign up voluntarily, it means they trust you enough to invite you into their inbox. This trust translates into higher open rates, click-through rates, and ultimately, conversions. Engaged subscribers are more likely to interact with your content, participate in your promotions, and make purchases. Moreover, permission-based marketing reduces bounce rates. Emails sent to interested recipients are less likely to bounce, ensuring that your messages reach their intended audience. This also improves your sender reputation, which is critical for maintaining high deliverability rates.

Growing your email list organically might seem like a slow process, but it's far more rewarding in the long run. One effective strategy is offering valuable lead magnets. Think of these as little gifts in exchange for an email address. E-books and whitepapers are popular choices, providing in-depth information on topics relevant to your audience. Webinars and online courses offer interactive learning experiences, making them highly attractive. Exclusive discounts and offers can also entice sign-ups, especially if they're time-sensitive. Free trials and samples are another great way to attract subscribers who are genuinely interested in your products or services.

Sign-up forms are your primary tool for capturing email addresses, so it's essential to optimize them for maximum conversions. Keep your forms short and simple. The fewer fields you ask for, the higher the likelihood that people will complete them. Use compelling call-to-action buttons that clearly state the benefit of signing up. Instead of a generic "Subscribe" button, try something more enticing like "Get Your Free Guide Now." Place these forms strategically on your website. Pop-ups can be effective when used sparingly and with proper timing. Consider placing forms on landing pages, in the footer, or within blog posts where they're relevant.

Promoting your sign-up opportunities is just as important as creating them. Leverage your social media platforms to drive traffic to your sign-up forms. Share links in your posts, stories, and bio sections. Include sign-up links in your blog posts to catch readers who are already engaged with your content. Referral programs can also be highly effective. Incentivize your current subscribers to refer friends by offering rewards in exchange. Partnering with influencers can expand your reach even further. They can promote your sign-up forms to their followers, providing a trusted recommendation that can significantly boost your list growth.

Compliance with email marketing regulations like GDPR and CAN-SPAM is non-negotiable. Including consent checkboxes ensures that subscribers knowingly opt-in, protecting you from legal issues. Providing clear privacy policies builds trust and transparency, reassuring subscribers that their data is safe. Make it easy for people to opt-out if they choose. A straightforward unsubscribe process not only keeps you compliant but also maintains a clean and engaged list.

Regularly maintaining and cleaning your email list is vital for keeping it high-quality. Start by removing inactive subscribers who haven't engaged with your emails in a long time. Use email verification tools to ensure that the addresses on your list are valid and active. Segment your list based on engagement levels. This allows you to tailor your messages to different segments, keeping your content relevant and maximizing engagement. Regular list cleaning improves your deliverability rates and ensures that your emails reach people who are genuinely interested in your brand.

Crafting Effective Email Campaigns

Creating an effective email campaign is like cooking a gourmet meal. Each element adds flavor, texture, and satisfaction, ensuring your audience returns for more. The first ingredient is an attention-grabbing subject line. This is your email's first impression, so make it count. A compelling subject line can be the difference between an email that gets opened and one that gets ignored. Use personalization to make it feel tailored. For example, including the recipient's name can grab their attention right away. Creating a sense of urgency can also be impactful. Phrases like "Limited Time Offer" or "Act Now" can prompt immediate action. Keep it concise and clear; a subject line that's too long might get cut off, especially on mobile devices. A/B testing can help you find the most effective subject lines. Try different variations and see which ones get the highest open rates.

The next essential element is a clear and compelling call-to-action (CTA). Your CTA is what you want your reader to do next, whether it's to click a link, download a resource, or make a purchase. Make sure your CTA stands out. Use action-oriented language like "Shop Now," "Download Free Guide," or "Sign Up Today." The CTA should be easy to find, preferably above the fold, so the reader doesn't have to scroll to see it. A strong CTA not only guides the reader but also increases your click-through rates, driving more traffic to your website or landing page.

Designing visually appealing emails is crucial for capturing and maintaining the reader's interest. A cluttered or unattractive email can turn people off, leading them to delete it without reading. Use a clean, logical layout with a clear hierarchy. Break up text with images and videos to make the content more engaging. Ensure your design is responsive, meaning it looks good on both desktop and mobile devices. More than half of all emails are opened on mobile devices, so this step cannot be overlooked. Test your emails on various devices and email clients to ensure they display correctly everywhere.

Personalized content can make your emails feel like a conversation rather than a broadcast. Use recipient data to tailor the content to their interests and behaviors. This could be anything from recommending products based on past purchases to sending birthday discounts. Keep the message clear and concise. Long-winded emails can lose the reader's interest quickly. Aim to get your main points across in the first few sentences. Strong visuals and interactive elements like buttons, GIFs, or polls can also enhance engagement.

Timing and frequency play a vital role in the success of your email campaigns. You don't want to overwhelm your subscribers with too many emails, but you also don't want to be forgotten by sending too few. Analyzing subscriber behavior can give you insights into the optimal times to send your emails. For instance, some studies suggest that emails sent on Tuesday mornings tend to perform well. However, this can vary based on your audience. A/B testing different send times can help you find what works best for your specific subscriber base. Be mindful of frequency. Sending too many emails can result in higher unsubscribe rates. Aim for a balance that keeps your audience engaged but not annoyed.

Incorporating all these elements into your email campaigns can boost your conversion and engagement rates. A well-crafted email campaign is not just about sending messages; it's about building relationships. By focusing on attention-grabbing subject lines, clear CTAs, visually appealing design, personalized content, and optimal timing and frequency, you can create emails that not only get opened but also drive action.

Segmenting Your Audience for Better Results

Segmenting your email list is like tailoring a suit, it ensures the perfect fit. When you send out emails, you want them to resonate with your audience. By segmenting your list, you can achieve higher engagement and conversions. Why is this so crucial? It's all about relevance. When your content matches the interests of different audience segments, it's more likely to be opened and clicked. This leads to higher open and click-through rates, which are direct indicators of your campaign's success. Improved customer satisfaction is another benefit. When subscribers receive content that feels personalized and relevant, they're more likely to engage and less likely to hit that dreaded unsubscribe button.

There are multiple ways to segment your email list, and each has its own set of advantages. Demographic information is a straightforward but powerful criterion. Age, gender, and location can significantly influence how a message is received. For example, a winter clothing sale might be more relevant to subscribers in colder regions. Behavioral data is another goldmine. This includes purchase history and website activity. If a subscriber has recently bought a product, sending them related product recommendations can be highly effective. Email engagement data, like opens, clicks, and inactivity, can also guide your segmentation. For instance, re-engagement campaigns can target subscribers who haven't opened your emails in a while, offering them special incentives to come back.

Creating segmented email campaigns involves more than just dividing your list; it's about creating messages that speak directly to each segment. Personalized product recommendations are a great way to start. If you know a segment of your audience has purchased a particular product, recommend complementary items. Targeted offers and discounts can also drive conversions. For example, offer a special discount to frequent buyers to reward their loyalty. Customized content based on interests can make your emails feel like they were written just for the recipient. If you have data showing a segment is interested in a specific topic, tailor your content to that interest. This not only boosts engagement but also builds a stronger connection with your audience.

***

Let's look at a real-world example to illustrate the power of segmentation.

> Consider a mid-sized online bookstore that wanted to boost its email marketing performance. They started by segmenting their list based on demographic information, purchase history, and email engagement. For demographics, they created segments like young adults, parents, and retirees. They also looked at behavioral data, identifying frequent buyers and those who engaged with specific genres like mystery or self-help.

Email engagement segments included active readers who opened most emails and inactive subscribers who hadn't engaged in months.   The bookstore implemented tailored strategies for each segment. For young adults, they sent emails featuring popular young adult novels and new releases. Parents received recommendations for children's books and educational materials. Retirees got content focused on bestsellers and classics. Frequent buyers received personalized product recommendations and exclusive discounts. They also ran re-engagement campaigns for inactive subscribers, offering a special discount to entice them back. The results were impressive. Open rates increased by 25%, and click-through rates saw a 30% boost. Sales from email campaigns went up by 20%, showing the effectiveness of their segmented approach.

The key takeaway here is the importance of understanding your audience on a deeper level. By segmenting your list and creating tailored campaigns, you can achieve higher engagement, improved customer satisfaction, and better conversions. This approach ensures that your emails are not just another message in the inbox but a valuable and relevant communication that your subscribers look forward to.

***

A/B Testing Your Email Campaigns

A/B testing, or split testing, is a technique where you compare two versions of an email to see which one performs better. This method allows you to make data-driven decisions, ensuring that your email campaigns are optimized for the best results. Imagine you have two subject lines but aren't sure which one will capture your audience's attention. By testing both, you can identify which resonates more and drives higher open rates. Data-driven decision-making is important because it takes the guesswork out of your marketing efforts. Instead of relying on intuition, you use hard data to understand what works best for your audience, leading to more effective campaigns.

So, what elements of an email can you A/B test? Start with the subject lines. They're the first thing recipients see and play a big role in whether your email gets opened or ignored. You can test different lengths, tones, or the inclusion of emojis. Next, consider the email copy and length. Some audiences prefer short, snappy messages, while others might appreciate more detailed content. Testing different call-to-action (CTA) buttons is also beneficial. Experiment with the wording, color, and placement of your CTA to see what drives more clicks. Don't forget about images and visual elements. An email with a compelling image might perform better than one with plain text. Testing these elements can give you insights into what your audience prefers.

Setting up an A/B test involves several steps. First, define your assumptions and objectives. For example, you might assume that a subject line with a sense of urgency will drive more opens. Your objective could be to increase the open rate by 10%. Next, split your email list into test groups. Ensure that these groups are similar in terms of size and demographics to avoid skewed results. Run the test by sending different versions of your email to these groups simultaneously. This helps eliminate variables that could affect the outcome, like the time of day. After running the test, collect and analyze the data. Look at key metrics such as open rates, click-through rates, and conversions. Implement changes based on your findings. If one version significantly outperforms the other, use those insights to optimize future emails.

Following best practices is essential for accurate and reliable A/B testing. First, test only one variable at a time. If you test multiple variables simultaneously, it's impossible to determine which one influenced the results. Make sure you have a large enough sample size to achieve statistical significance. Testing with too small a group can lead to inconclusive results. Run your tests for an appropriate duration. Ending a test too early might not give you a complete picture. Continuously test and adjust. The digital landscape is ever-changing, and what works today might not work tomorrow. Regular testing helps you stay ahead of the curve and adapt to your audience's evolving preferences.

Effective A/B testing is a powerful tool in your email marketing strategy. By understanding what elements resonate with your audience, you can create more engaging and effective email campaigns. Whether it's tweaking subject lines, refining your email copy, or experimenting with different CTAs, A/B testing provides the insights needed to optimize your efforts. Regular testing and adjustment ensure that your campaigns remain relevant and impactful, driving better results and higher engagement rates.

Analyzing and Improving Email Performance

Understanding the importance of data interpretation is essential for anyone serious about email marketing. Imagine you're on a road trip without GPS. You might be moving, but you have no idea if you're heading in the right direction. Data acts as your GPS, guiding you to make informed adjustments. By interpreting data correctly, you can identify strengths and weaknesses in your campaigns. For instance, if you notice that your open rates are high, but click-through rates are low, it might indicate that while your subject lines are compelling, the content inside your emails needs work. This kind of insight allows you to tweak your strategy and improve overall performance.

Key metrics to track are your bread and butter in email marketing. Open rate is a primary indicator of how well your subject lines are performing. It shows the percentage of recipients who open your email. A low open rate could signal that your subject lines aren't enticing enough or that your emails are landing in spam folders. Click-through rate (CTR) is next on the list. This metric reveals how many recipients clicked on one or more links in your email. A high CTR indicates that your content is engaging and relevant. Conversion rate goes a step further by showing how many of those clicks resulted in a desired action, like making a purchase. Bounce rate measures the percentage of emails that couldn't be delivered. A high bounce rate can damage your sender reputation. Lastly, the unsubscribe rate tells you how many recipients opted out of your email list after receiving a campaign. Monitoring these metrics gives you a comprehensive view of your email performance.

Using analytics tools is a game-changer for tracking and analyzing email performance. Platforms like Mailchimp and Constant Contact offer built-in analytics that provide detailed reports on various metrics. These tools make it easy to see how your emails are performing at a glance. Integrating Google Analytics with your email marketing platform can offer even deeper insights. You can track user behavior on your website after they click through from an email, giving you a better understanding of the customer journey. Custom tracking and reporting tools allow for more tailored insights. You can set up specific goals and track their progress, making it easier to measure the success of your campaigns.

Interpreting data and identifying trends is where the magic happens. Analyzing metrics over time helps you see the bigger picture. For example, if you notice a gradual decline in open rates, it might be time to refresh your subject lines or review your sending frequency. Comparing performance across different campaigns can highlight what works best for your audience. Maybe your holiday promotions always perform better than your regular newsletters. Identifying patterns and areas for improvement allows you to fine-tune your strategy continuously. Look for recurring trends, like which types of subject lines or content formats get the most engagement, and use that information to shape future campaigns.

Continuous improvement strategies are essential for keeping your email marketing efforts fresh and effective. Implementing changes based on A/B test results is a practical way to optimize your campaigns. If you discover that a particular subject line drives higher open rates, apply similar styles to future emails. Regularly updating and testing email templates ensures that your design stays modern and user-friendly. Soliciting feedback from subscribers can provide valuable insights. Ask them what they like or dislike about your emails and use that information to make improvements. Staying updated with email marketing best practices is also essential. The digital landscape is always evolving, and what worked last year might not be as effective today. Keep an eye on industry trends and adapt accordingly.

In summary, analyzing and improving email performance is a continuous process that involves making informed adjustments, tracking key metrics, using analytics tools, interpreting data, and implementing continuous improvement strategies. This approach ensures that your email marketing efforts remain effective and aligned with your goals. Next, we'll explore how to harness content marketing for effectiveness across all platforms and strategies.

Make a Difference with Your Review

"Kindness is the key to happiness. The more we share, the more we grow."
- Unknown

People who give without expectation live longer, happier lives, and make more money. So if we've got a shot at that during our time together, I'm gonna try. To make that happen, I have a question for you... Would you help someone you've never met, even if you never got credit for it?

Who is this person you ask? They are like you. Or, at least, like you used to be. Less experienced, wanting to make a difference, and needing help, but not sure where to look.

Our mission is to make mastering of digital marketing accessible to everyone. Everything we do stems from that mission. And, the only way for us to accomplish that mission is by reaching...well...everyone.

This is where you come in. Most people do, in fact, judge a book by its cover (and its reviews). So here's my ask on behalf of a struggling marketer you've never met: Please help that aspiring digital marketer master by leaving this book a review. Your gift costs no money and less than 60 seconds to make real, but can change a fellow reader's life forever. Your review could help... one more small business provide for their community. ...one more marketer support their family... one more dream come true.

To get that 'feel good' feeling and help this person for real, all you have to do is...and it takes less than 60 seconds...leave a review.

Simply scan the QR code below to leave your review:

If you feel good about helping a faceless marketer, you are my kind of person. Welcome to the club. You're one of us. Thank you from the bottom of my heart. Now, back to our regularly scheduled programming. – Your biggest fan, Waldo's Publishing Company

Chapter Six

Content Marketing for Engagement and Growth

Content marketing is like hosting a dinner party. You want your guests to enjoy themselves, feel engaged, and leave with something valuable. Whether you're a business owner or just starting out, the right content strategy can be a game-changer. It's not just about creating content; it's about creating the right content for the right people. Let's dive in and set the table for success.

Developing a Content Marketing Strategy

The process for developing a successful content marketing strategy relies on the same pillars we have previously discussed; Defining Goals, Identifying your Target Audience, Auditing your Strategy, and your Content Calendar. Here is a quick overview of these pillars before diving into content creation.

Define Your Content Marketing Goals: Your content marketing goals should be well-defined. Are you looking to increase brand awareness? Generate leads? Improve customer engagement? Each goal requires a different approach. For instance, if your goal is to increase brand awareness, you might focus on creating shareable content like infographics and blog posts. If generating leads is your aim, gated content like eBooks and webinars could be more effective. Aligning your content goals with your overall marketing objectives is essential for success. For example, if your business objective is to expand into a new market, your content goal could be to "increase brand awareness in the new market by 30% in six months." This ensures that your content efforts are not just random acts but are strategically contributing to your broader aims.

Identify Your Target Audience: Creating detailed buyer personas is a key tool in this process. As it includes demographic information, behaviors, interests, and pain points, which are the key components to understanding your audience. Conducting audience research through surveys and social media listening provides valuable insights. Surveys can ask direct questions about your audience's preferences and challenges. Social media listening involves monitoring what people are saying about your brand and industry online. This can reveal trends and sentiments that help you understand your audience better. Knowing your audience inside out allows you to create content that resonates with them, making your marketing efforts more effective.

Content Audit and Gap Analysis: This process starts by listing all existing content. This includes blog posts, videos, social media updates, and more. Once you have a comprehensive list, analyze the performance metrics of each piece. Look at metrics like traffic, engagement, and conversion rates. This helps you understand what's working and what's not. Identifying content gaps and opportunities is the next step. Maybe you have plenty of blog posts but lack video content. Or perhaps your content doesn't cover certain topics that are important to your audience. For instance, if you're a tech company, you might discover that you have plenty of product reviews but not enough how-to guides. Identifying these gaps allows you to create new content that fills them, making your overall strategy more robust.

Content Plan and Editorial Calendar: A content plan outlines what content you will create, who will create it, and how it will be distributed. It should include details like topics, formats, and publication dates. For example, if you're a travel agency, your plan might include blog posts about travel tips, destination guides, and customer testimonials. An editorial calendar helps you stay organized and consistent. It ensures that you're posting regularly and covering all necessary topics. Schedule content around key dates and events relevant to your industry. For instance, if you're a retail brand, plan content around major shopping holidays like Black Friday and Christmas. This not only keeps your content timely but also helps you stay ahead of important dates.

By setting clear goals, understanding your audience, auditing your content, and planning meticulously, you can create a content marketing strategy that truly engages and grows your audience.

Crafting Engaging and Shareable Content

Creating content that truly engages and gets shared is like baking a cake. You need the right ingredients and a bit of flair. First off, your content must be relevant and valuable to your audience. Think about the problems your audience faces and how your content can solve them. For example, if you're running a fitness blog, articles on quick workout routines for busy professionals will hit home. People share content that adds value to their lives, so always aim to inform, entertain, or inspire.

Emotional appeal is another key ingredient. Content that tugs at the heartstrings, makes people laugh, or sparks curiosity has a higher chance of being shared. Emotional content resonates on a personal level, making people want to share it with their friends and family. Consider a heartfelt customer testimonial or a behind-the-scenes look at your team's community service efforts. These kinds of stories don't just promote your brand; they build a connection with your audience. When people feel something, they're more likely to act, whether that's clicking, sharing, or buying.

Visual elements are the final touch that can make your content stand out. In a world where people are constantly bombarded with information, eye-catching visuals can grab attention and make your content more engaging. High-quality images, infographics, and videos can break up text and make your content easier to digest. For instance, a well-designed infographic can convey complex information quickly and clearly. Videos add another layer of engagement, allowing you to explain topics more deeply or showcase your products in action. Even simple images can make a blog post more enjoyable to read.

To ensure your content has these characteristics, always start with your audience in mind. Use tools like Google Analytics and social media insights to understand what your audience is interested in. Create content that addresses their pain points, answers their questions, and entertains them. Incorporate emotional storytelling to make your content more relatable and memorable. Use high-quality visuals to enhance your message and keep your audience engaged. By focusing on relevance, emotional appeal, and visual elements, you can craft content that not only engages but also gets shared, extending your reach and impact.

Writing Compelling Blog Posts

Choosing blog topics that resonate with your audience is like picking the right ingredients for a tasty dish. You want to make sure you're catering to their tastes and needs. Start by using keyword research tools to identify popular topics. Tools like Google Keyword Planner or SEMrush can help you find what people are searching for in your niche. Analyzing competitors' content is another smart move. See what topics they're covering and how well those posts are performing. It's not about copying but understanding what works. Addressing common customer questions and pain points can also guide your topic selection. If customers frequently ask about a specific issue, that's a goldmine for your blog content.

Crafting engaging headlines is an art. Your headline is the first thing readers see, and it needs to grab their attention immediately. Using numbers and lists is a proven strategy. Headlines like "10 Tips for Better Sleep" or "5 Ways to Boost Your Productivity" are eye-catching and promise actionable insights. Incorporating power words and emotional triggers can make your headlines even more compelling. Words like "ultimate," "essential," and "proven" add weight, while emotional triggers like "amazing" or "heartbreaking" evoke curiosity. Keeping headlines concise and specific ensures they are clear and to the point. A good rule of thumb is to aim for headlines under 60 characters. This makes them easy to read and less likely to get cut off in search results.

Creating valuable content is the heart of blogging. Your posts should offer actionable advice and tips that readers can implement. This not only provides value but also establishes your authority on the subject. Using data and statistics to support your arguments adds credibility. For instance, if you're writing about the benefits of remote work, citing studies on productivity can strengthen your case. Including real-world examples and case studies makes your content relatable and practical. Share stories from your own experience or highlight success stories from others in your industry. This not only makes your content more engaging but also shows that your advice works in real-life scenarios.

Optimizing your blog posts for SEO is crucial for visibility. Start by using primary and secondary keywords naturally throughout your content. Avoid keyword stuffing; instead, integrate them seamlessly into your sentences. Adding internal and external links enriches your content and improves SEO. Internal links guide readers to other relevant posts on your site, keeping them engaged longer. External links to reputable sources add value and credibility to your content. Don't forget to optimize images with alternative text and descriptive file names. Using these on-page SEO best practices ensures your blog posts are both user-friendly and search engine-friendly.

Creating High-Quality Video Content

Planning your video content is like setting the stage for a play. You need a clear vision of what you want to achieve and how you plan to get there. Start by outlining the video's purpose and key messages. Are you aiming to educate, entertain, or promote a product? Knowing this helps you stay focused. Creating a storyboard is your next step. This visual plan outlines each scene, helping you visualize the flow and structure. It's like a comic strip that guides your filming process. Writing a detailed script is also important. This isn't just about what's said; it includes directions for actions, camera angles, and any on-screen text. A well-written script ensures everyone knows their role and reduces the chances of mistakes during filming.

When it comes to production, the right equipment can make or break your video. You don't need the most expensive gear, but investing in good-quality cameras, microphones, and lighting is helpful. A clear, sharp image and crisp audio can significantly enhance your video's professionalism. Setting up an appropriate filming location is also important. Choose a quiet, well-lit space that matches the video's tone and message. For example, a cozy, well-decorated kitchen might be perfect for a cooking tutorial. Ensuring good audio and video quality is non-negotiable. Background noise, poor lighting, or shaky footage can distract viewers and diminish your message. Use tripods to stabilize your camera and consider using external microphones for better sound quality.

Editing and post-production are where your raw footage transforms into a polished final product. Using editing software like Adobe Premiere or Final Cut Pro allows you to cut unnecessary parts, rearrange clips, and add transitions. Adding graphics, text overlays, and call-to-actions can enhance your video's clarity and engagement. For instance, a text overlay can highlight key points, while a call-to-action can prompt viewers to visit your website or subscribe to your channel. Incorporating music and sound effects adds another layer of professionalism. Background music can set the mood, while sound effects can emphasize important moments. However, be mindful not to overdo it. The goal is to complement your content, not overshadow it.

Promoting your video content is just as important as creating it. Share your videos across various social media channels like YouTube, Facebook, and Instagram to reach a wider audience. Each platform has its unique strengths, so tailor your promotion strategies accordingly. Embedding videos in blog posts and emails can drive traffic and keep your audience engaged. For example, a video embedded in a blog post can provide a visual explanation of the topic, while an email with a video can increase click-through rates. Encouraging viewers to share and comment can also boost your video's visibility. Ask questions or include prompts in your video to encourage interaction. The more engagement your video gets, the more likely it is to be seen by a larger audience.

Leveraging User-Generated Content

User-Generated Content (UGC) can be a game-changer for your brand's content marketing efforts. Think of UGC as the digital equivalent of word-of-mouth recommendations. It builds trust and authenticity because it comes directly from your customers. When people see others using and loving your products, they're more likely to trust your brand. This kind of content also increases engagement and interaction. People love sharing their experiences, and when they do, it fosters a community around your brand. Plus, UGC can significantly expand your reach. When someone posts about your product, their entire network sees it, introducing your brand to potential new customers who might not have found you otherwise.

Encouraging your customers and followers to create and share content requires a bit of strategy. Running social media contests and challenges can be very effective. For example, ask your followers to share photos of themselves using your product with a specific hashtag for a chance to win a prize. This not only generates content but also creates excitement around your brand. Creating branded hashtags is another great way to encourage UGC. A catchy, unique hashtag can inspire your customers to share their experiences. Offering incentives like discounts or features on your brand's social media can also motivate people to share. When customers know they might get a shout-out or a special deal, they're more likely to participate.

Curating and sharing UGC involves a few key steps. First, select high-quality and relevant content. Not every post will be a fit for your brand's image, so choose wisely. Look for content that aligns with your brand's values and aesthetic. Always ask for permission before sharing someone else's content. A simple message asking for their approval can go a long way in building goodwill. Once you have the green light, make sure to tag and credit the original creators. This not only gives them recognition but also encourages more people to create and share content in hopes of being featured. Properly crediting creators also shows respect for their work, which can strengthen your relationship with your audience.

Integrating UGC into your marketing campaigns can amplify your efforts. Featuring UGC in your social media posts and stories can make your content more relatable and engaging. People love seeing real-life examples of others using your products. Using UGC in email marketing campaigns can also be effective. For instance, include customer photos or testimonials in your newsletters to add a personal touch. Showcasing UGC on your brand's website is another powerful strategy. Create a dedicated section for customer photos and stories. This not only adds authenticity but also provides social proof, showing potential customers that real people love your products. By leveraging UGC across various channels, you can create a more engaging and authentic brand experience.

Content Repurposing: Maximizing Your Efforts

Content repurposing is a game-changer for maximizing your content marketing efforts. Think of it as recycling but for your content. Instead of constantly creating new material, you extend the lifespan of existing content by giving it a fresh twist. This strategy not only saves time and resources but also helps you reach new audiences who might have missed the original. For example, a well-performing blog post can be transformed into a video or a series of social media posts. This way, you get more mileage out of your content and ensure it continues to provide value.

Identifying which content to repurpose is the first step. Start by analyzing your top-performing blog posts. These are the pieces that have already proven their worth by attracting traffic and engaging readers. Evergreen content, which remains relevant over time, is another goldmine. Topics like "how-to" guides or industry best practices often fall into this category. Additionally, consider audience feedback and questions. If a particular post has generated a lot of comments or inquiries, it's a sign that the topic resonates with your audience and could be repurposed into other formats for even greater impact.

There are various methods to repurpose content effectively. Turning blog posts into videos or podcasts is a popular approach. For instance, a detailed blog post on digital marketing strategies can be adapted into a video tutorial, providing a visual and auditory experience for your audience. Creating infographics from data-heavy articles is another effective method. Infographics break down complex information into visually appealing, easy-to-digest graphics. Developing eBooks or whitepapers from a series of related posts can also add significant value. These comprehensive resources can serve as lead magnets, attracting new subscribers and generating leads. Lastly, sharing snippets and quotes on social media keeps your presence active and engages your audience with bite-sized pieces of valuable content.

Promoting repurposed content ensures it reaches a wide audience. Cross-promoting on different platforms is a must. Share your newly created videos on YouTube, embed them in related blog posts, and post them on social media. Use email newsletters to highlight repurposed content. For example, include a section in your newsletter that features a new infographic or a link to your latest podcast episode. Collaborating with influencers to share repurposed content can also amplify your reach. Influencers can introduce your content to their established audiences, providing credibility and attracting new followers.

In summary, content repurposing is a powerful strategy for extending the life of your content, reaching new audiences, and saving valuable time and resources. By identifying high-potential content, using various repurposing methods, and effectively promoting your revamped material, you can maximize your content marketing efforts and keep your audience engaged. This sets the stage for the next chapter, where we'll explore how to harness data analytics to optimize your digital marketing strategies further.

Chapter Seven

Harnessing the Power of Data Analytics

Ever feel like you're flying blind with your digital marketing efforts? Imagine trying to hit a target in the dark without knowing if your aim is on point. That's what it's like when you're not using data analytics to guide your decisions. Data analytics shines a light on your performance, showing you what's working and what needs tweaking. For business owners, marketing professionals, and beginners alike, understanding and leveraging data can be a game-changer. Let's dive into how Google Analytics can illuminate your path.

Introduction to Google Analytics

Google Analytics is a powerful tool designed to track and analyze your website's performance. Think of it as the control center for your digital marketing spaceship. It provides a wealth of information about how visitors interact with your site, which pages they visit, how long they stay, and much more. This data is invaluable for optimizing your website and making informed marketing decisions.

Using Google Analytics is pivotal in digital marketing. It helps you understand your audience's behavior, track the effectiveness of your campaigns, and measure your return on investment (ROI). With this tool, you can see where your traffic is coming from, what content resonates most with your audience, and how visitors navigate your site.

This insight allows you to fine-tune your strategies and improve your overall marketing performance.

Google Analytics boasts a range of features and capabilities. It tracks key metrics like sessions, users, pageviews, bounce rate, and average session duration. You can set up goals to track specific actions, such as form submissions or purchases, and use e-commerce tracking to measure sales performance. The tool offers detailed reports on audience demographics, traffic sources, user behavior, and conversions. Additionally, Google Analytics 4 (GA4) leverages machine learning to provide predictive insights and deeper analysis.

Setting up Google Analytics is straightforward, even if you're not a tech wizard. Start by creating a Google Analytics account. Go to the Google Analytics website and sign up using your Google account. Once you're in, create a new property for your website. You'll be prompted to enter basic details like your website name, URL, industry category, and time zone. Next, you need to add the tracking code to your website. Google Analytics provides a unique tracking ID that you need to insert into the HTML of your site. If you're using a content management system like WordPress, there are plugins that make this process easier. Don't forget to configure basic settings, such as your time zone and currency, to ensure accurate reporting.

With the introduction of Google Analytics 4 (GA4), the setup process has evolved. GA4 offers enhanced tracking capabilities and a more flexible data model compared to its predecessor, Universal Analytics. To set up GA4, follow the same initial steps as creating an account and property. Then, you'll need to create a data stream for your website. This involves providing the URL and configuring additional settings like enhanced measurement, which automatically tracks events such as pageviews, scrolls, and outbound clicks. You can install the GA4 tracking code using Google Tag Manager, a website builder integration, or manually adding it to your site's code.

Navigating the Google Analytics interface might seem daunting at first, but it becomes second nature with a bit of practice. The Home dashboard offers a snapshot of your site's performance, including metrics like active users, top pages, and traffic sources. It's your quick reference guide for overall health. The Real-Time data section shows live activity on your site, providing instant insights into how users are interacting at that moment. This is particularly useful during campaign launches or special promotions.

Audience reports delve into the demographics and interests of your visitors. You can see age, gender, location, and even affinity categories that indicate user interests. This data helps tailor your content and marketing efforts to better match your audience. Acquisition reports reveal where your traffic is coming from, whether it's organic search, social media, or paid campaigns. Understanding these sources helps you allocate your marketing budget more effectively. Behavior reports focus on user interactions with your site. You can see which pages are most popular, how users navigate between pages, and where they drop off. Conversion reports track the completion of specific goals, such as form submissions or purchases, giving you a clear picture of your site's effectiveness in driving desired actions.

Key reports and metrics in Google Analytics are essential for understanding your website's performance. The Audience, Acquisition, Behavior, and Conversion reports each offer unique insights. Sessions indicate the number of individual visits to your site, while users represent unique visitors. Pageviews show how many times a page is viewed, and the bounce rate indicates the percentage of visitors who leave after viewing only one page. Average session duration measures how long visitors stay on your site. Customizing and saving reports allows you to focus on the metrics that matter most to your business. You can create custom dashboards that aggregate key metrics, set up alerts for significant changes, and even share reports with your team to keep everyone aligned.

Using Google Analytics effectively transforms raw data into actionable insights. By understanding your audience, tracking campaign performance, and optimizing your website, you can make informed decisions that drive growth and success. Whether you're a seasoned marketer or just starting out, mastering Google Analytics is a crucial step in harnessing the power of data analytics for your business.

Setting Up and Tracking KPIs

Understanding KPIs in digital marketing is like having a map for a road trip. You wouldn't start a trip without knowing your destination and the best route to get there. Key Performance Indicators (KPIs) are the quantifiable measures that help you track your progress, measure success, and guide future strategies. They provide a clear picture of how your marketing efforts are performing and whether you're on track to meet your goals. For instance, common digital marketing KPIs include conversion rate, return on ad spend (ROAS), customer lifetime value (CLV), and various traffic and engagement metrics such as website visits, page views, social shares, and comments. Each KPI serves a specific purpose, helping you focus on what matters most to your business.

Identifying the right KPIs starts with aligning them with your marketing objectives. If your goal is lead generation, KPIs like conversion rate and cost per lead (CPL) will be what to focus on. For brand awareness, you might focus on metrics like social media engagement and website traffic. Differentiating between leading and lagging indicators is also important. Leading indicators, like website traffic and social media engagement, show early signs of success, while lagging indicators, such as revenue and CLV, reflect long-term outcomes. Setting realistic and achievable targets for each KPI ensures that your goals are attainable and keeps your team motivated. For example, aiming for a 5% increase in conversion rate over three months is both challenging and achievable.

Setting up KPI tracking in Google Analytics involves configuring the platform to monitor specific actions that align with your goals. Start by setting up goals and events. Goals track specific actions users take on your site, like completing a purchase or signing up for a newsletter. Events are more granular actions, such as button clicks or video plays. To set these up, navigate to the Admin section in Google Analytics, select Goals, and follow the prompts to define each goal. For e-commerce tracking, you'll need to enable e-commerce settings and add additional tracking code to your site. This allows you to track transactions, revenue, and product performance. Using custom dimensions and metrics lets you capture data unique to your business. For example, you might track user type (new vs. returning) or content type (blog vs. product page). Integrating Google Analytics with other tools like Google Ads and CRM systems provides a holistic view of your marketing performance, enabling you to track the entire customer journey from ad click to sale.

Monitoring and reporting on KPIs is an ongoing process that involves regular analysis and adjustments. Creating custom dashboards and reports in Google Analytics helps you focus on the most important metrics. Dashboards provide a snapshot of key KPIs, allowing you to monitor performance at a glance. You can customize these dashboards to include metrics that matter most to your business. Automating reports with tools like Google Data Studio saves time and ensures you get consistent updates on your metrics. Data Studio allows you to create visually appealing reports that pull data directly from Google Analytics, making it easy to share insights with your team. Analyzing trends and patterns over time helps you understand what's working and what's not. Look for patterns in your data, such as seasonal fluctuations or spikes in traffic after a campaign launch. Sharing insights and recommendations with stakeholders ensures everyone is on the same page and can make informed decisions. Regularly presenting your findings in team meetings keeps everyone aligned and focused on the right objectives.

In Google Analytics, you can create a custom dashboard that tracks essential KPIs like conversion rate, average session duration, and bounce rate. This dashboard provides a quick overview of how your site is performing and highlights areas needing improvement. For example, if you notice a high bounce rate on a specific page, you can investigate further to understand why visitors are leaving and make necessary adjustments. Automating reports with Google Data Studio takes this a step further by allowing you to create detailed, interactive reports that update in real-time. These reports can be shared with your team and stakeholders, providing a transparent view of your marketing performance. Analyzing trends and patterns over time helps you identify what's working and where you need to pivot. For instance, if you see a consistent increase in traffic from social media, you might decide to allocate more resources to that channel. Sharing insights and recommendations with your team ensures everyone is aligned and working towards the same goals. Regularly reviewing and discussing these insights keeps your strategy dynamic and responsive to changes in performance.

Analyzing Traffic Sources

Understanding where your website traffic comes from is like knowing the different routes customers take to reach your store. Each path offers unique insights and opportunities. Let's break down the main traffic sources: direct traffic, organic search traffic, paid search traffic, referral traffic, social media traffic, and email traffic.

- Direct traffic: consists of visitors who type your URL directly into their browser or use bookmarks. This type of traffic often indicates brand loyalty and familiarity.

- Organic search traffic: comes from search engines like Google, without any ads involved. It's driven by your website's SEO efforts.

- Paid search traffic: is generated through PPC campaigns where you pay for each click.

- Referral traffic: are visitors who come to your site from links on other websites.

- Social media traffic: comes from platforms like Facebook, Instagram, and LinkedIn.

- Email traffic: is generated from email marketing campaigns, such as newsletters and promotional emails.

Using Google Analytics to analyze these traffic sources is straightforward. Start by accessing the Acquisition reports. This section provides a comprehensive overview of how visitors find your website. Navigate to the Channels Report to see a breakdown of traffic by source. This report categorizes traffic into channels like organic search, direct, referral, and social. Understanding the Source/Medium report gives you a more detailed view, combining specific sources (like Google or Facebook) with their mediums (organic, paid, etc.). This helps you identify the exact origin of your traffic. The Referrals report is particularly useful for tracking referral traffic. It shows which websites are sending visitors to your site, allowing you to identify valuable partnerships and backlinks.

Evaluating the quality of traffic from different sources involves looking at key metrics; bounce rate, average session duration, pager per session, and conversion rate. By analyzing these metrics, you can determine which traffic sources bring the most engaged and valuable visitors.

- Bounce rate: indicates the percentage of visitors who leave after viewing only one page. A high bounce rate could suggest that your landing page isn't engaging or relevant.

- Average session duration: measures how long visitors stay on your site. Longer sessions typically indicate higher engagement.

- Pages per session: shows how many pages a visitor views in one visit. More pages suggest that visitors are exploring your content.

- Conversion rate: is the ultimate metric, showing the percentage of visitors who complete a desired action, like making a purchase.

Optimizing traffic sources based on analysis can significantly improve your marketing effectiveness. For organic search traffic, focus on enhancing your SEO efforts. This includes optimizing your website content for relevant keywords, improving site speed, and building high-quality backlinks. For paid search campaigns, regularly review and adjust your ad copy, keywords, and bidding strategies to ensure you're getting the best ROI. Building referral partnerships involves reaching out to authoritative websites in your industry and offering valuable content or collaborations that encourage them to link back to your site. Leveraging social media platforms requires creating engaging content tailored to each platform's audience. Use analytics to identify which types of posts perform best and focus on replicating that success.

For example, if you notice that a significant portion of your traffic comes from Instagram, you might invest more in high-quality visuals and stories that resonate with your audience. Similarly, if a blog post on a partner's site drives substantial referral traffic, consider creating more guest posts or collaborations with that partner. By continuously analyzing and optimizing your traffic sources, you can ensure that your website attracts high-quality visitors who are more likely to convert.

Keep in mind, the aim is not just to boost traffic, but to attract the right traffic. By understanding where your visitors come from and how they interact with your site, you can make informed decisions that drive meaningful results. Whether you're a seasoned marketer or just starting, mastering the analysis of traffic sources is a crucial step in your digital marketing journey.

Understanding User Behavior

Understanding user behavior on your website is like having a map of your visitors' journey, showing you exactly where they go, what catches their eye, and where they lose interest. Google Analytics offers several Behavior reports that help you get inside the minds of your users. The Behavior Flow Report is a visual representation of the paths users take through your site. It starts from the landing page and shows each step they take, making it easy to identify common entry and exit points. This report helps you see how users navigate your site and where they might drop off, providing valuable insights for improving user experience.

The Site Content reports are another goldmine of information. The All Pages report shows you data for every page on your site, including pageviews, unique pageviews, average time on page, and bounce rate. The Content Drilldown report breaks down your site's content structure, showing performance metrics for different sections or directories. The Landing Pages report focuses on the first page visitors see when they arrive at your site, which is vital for understanding first impressions. Lastly, the Exit Pages report shows you which pages users leave from, helping you identify potential issues or points of friction.

The Site Speed report is essential for understanding how your site's performance impacts user behavior. It provides data on page load times, breaking it down by browser, country, and page. Slow load times can frustrate users and lead to higher bounce rates, so this report helps you pinpoint areas for improvement. The Site Search report is invaluable if your site has a search function. It shows what users are searching for, revealing gaps in your content or areas where users struggle to find information.

Analyzing user behavior flow is like tracing the footsteps of your visitors. The Behavior Flow diagram in Google Analytics shows the journey users take from one page to another. By interpreting this diagram, you can see which paths are most common and where users tend to exit. Identifying these common entry and exit points helps you understand what draws users in and what might be driving them away. Analyzing drop-off points is particularly important. If you notice a significant number of users leaving from a specific page, it's a signal that something isn't working, maybe the content isn't engaging, or there's a technical issue. Understanding user journeys allows you to create a smoother, more intuitive experience that keeps visitors engaged.

Evaluating the performance of individual pages is critical for optimizing your site. Pageviews and unique pageviews show how many times a page is viewed and by how many individual users. Average time on page indicates how long visitors stay on a page, giving you an idea of how engaging the content is. Bounce rate measures the percentage of visitors who leave after viewing just one page. A high bounce rate might suggest that the page isn't meeting visitors' expectations. Exit rate shows the percentage of exits from a specific page, helping you identify potential problem areas. Analyzing top-performing pages can reveal what's working well, while identifying underperforming pages highlights areas needing improvement.

Using heatmaps and session recordings takes understanding user behavior to the next level. Tools like Hotjar, Crazy Egg, and Microsoft Clarity provide visual representations of where users click, how far they scroll, and what grabs their attention. Heatmaps show hot spots of activity, highlighting areas that get the most interaction. Analyzing click patterns can reveal if users are clicking on non-interactive elements, indicating a need for clearer design. Scroll depth shows how far down the page users go, helping you understand if your content is too long or if key information is being missed.

Watching session recordings is like looking over the shoulder of your visitors. These tools record real user sessions, allowing you to see exactly how they navigate your site. This can help identify usability issues, such as confusing navigation or broken links. Using these insights, you can make data-driven decisions to improve user experience. For example, if you notice users frequently abandoning their carts on an e-commerce site, you might streamline the checkout process or add more reassuring information about payment security.

Understanding user behavior through these tools and reports enables you to create a more engaging and user-friendly website. By continuously analyzing and optimizing based on real user data, you can improve your site's performance and drive better results for your business.

Using Data to Optimize Campaigns

Data-driven decision making is like having a crystal ball for your marketing efforts. It allows you to see what's working, what's not, and where to focus your resources. The benefits are enormous. By relying on data, you reduce guesswork and assumptions, making your campaigns more precise. This precision leads to improved campaign effectiveness and a higher return on investment (ROI). This approach not only saves time and money but also enhances your overall marketing performance.

Analyzing campaign performance using Google Analytics is straightforward. Start by accessing the Campaigns report, which provides insights into how your various marketing efforts are performing. This report shows metrics such as sessions, users, goal completions, and revenue. Sessions indicate the number of visits initiated by your campaigns, while users represent the unique visitors brought in. Goal completions track the specific actions users take, like signing up for a newsletter or making a purchase. Revenue metrics give you a clear picture of the financial impact of your campaigns.

Compare performance across different campaigns to identify which ones are hitting the mark and which are falling short. Look at metrics like conversion rates, cost per acquisition (CPA), and return on ad spend (ROAS). High-performing campaigns will show strong metrics across the board, while underperforming ones will reveal areas needing improvement. Identifying these successful and underperforming campaigns allows you to allocate resources more effectively, focusing on what works and tweaking what doesn't.

Once you've analyzed the data, it's time to optimize your campaigns. Start by adjusting your targeting and segmentation. If a particular audience segment is converting well, consider expanding your reach within that segment. Conversely, if another segment isn't performing, you might need to refine your targeting criteria. Next, refine your ad copy and creatives. Look at the ads with the highest click-through rates (CTR) and conversion rates. What elements are making them successful? Is it the headline, the imagery, or the call-to-action? Use these insights to improve your underperforming ads.

Allocating your budget to high-performing channels. If your data shows that social media ads are driving more conversions than search ads, consider shifting more of your budget towards social media. This ensures that you're investing in channels that deliver the best results. Testing and iterating on campaign elements is an ongoing process. Run A/B tests on different ad variations, landing pages, and CTAs to see what resonates best with your audience. Use the results to continually refine and improve your campaigns.

✳✳✳

Let's consider a real-world example.

> A mid-sized e-commerce business launched a multi-channel marketing campaign to boost holiday sales. Their initial campaign included social media ads, email marketing, and PPC ads. After running the campaign for a week, they used Google Analytics to analyze performance. They found that social media ads were driving the most traffic but had a high bounce rate. Email marketing, on the other hand, had lower traffic but higher conversion rates. Based on these insights, they decided to optimize their campaign. They adjusted their social media targeting to reach a more engaged audience and refined their ad copy to be more compelling. They also allocated more budget to email marketing, given its higher conversion rates. The results were impressive. By the end of the holiday season, they saw a 20% increase in sales compared to the previous year. Their social media bounce rate decreased by 15%, and their email marketing conversions increased by 25%.

The key takeaway here is the power of data-driven decision making. By analyzing their campaign performance and making informed adjustments, they were able to optimize their efforts and achieve remarkable results.

✳✳✳

Chapter Eight

Integrating AI and Emerging Technologies

I magine having a marketing assistant who never sleeps, never gets tired, and constantly learns from its experiences. This isn't a sci-fi movie; it's the reality of Artificial Intelligence (AI) in digital marketing today. As a business owner or beginner, you've likely heard the buzz around AI, but what does it really mean for you? Let's break it down.

The Role of AI in Digital Marketing

At its core, AI refers to machines that can mimic human intelligence. Machine learning, a subset of AI, involves algorithms that learn from data, making predictions or decisions without explicit programming for each task. For instance, when you see personalized recommendations on Netflix or Amazon, that's AI in action. In digital marketing, AI applications range from data analysis to customer insights, effectively turning raw data into actionable strategies. Imagine sifting through thousands of customer interactions to find patterns. AI can do that in seconds, providing insights that would take a human team days to uncover. This capability is crucial for understanding customer behavior and preferences.

AI also automates routine marketing tasks. Think about email segmentation, social media scheduling, or even ad placements. AI tools can handle these tasks efficiently, freeing you to focus on strategy and creativity. Beyond automation, AI enhances the customer experience through tools like chatbots and personalized content recommendations. These AI-driven tools can provide instant responses to customer queries, suggest relevant products, and even predict future customer needs based on past behaviors.

The benefits of integrating AI into your digital marketing strategy are immense. First, it improves efficiency and productivity. By automating repetitive tasks, AI allows your team to focus on more strategic initiatives. This means faster campaign deployments and quicker adjustments based on real-time data. AI also enhances personalization and targeting. With AI, you can create personalized marketing messages at scale. Whether it's dynamic email content or personalized product recommendations, AI ensures that your marketing efforts resonate with individual customers.

Real-time data processing and analysis are other significant advantages. AI can process vast amounts of data in real time, providing you with insights that are current and actionable. This capability is particularly useful for monitoring social media trends or tracking the performance of digital ads. Predictive analytics is another game-changer. Using historical data, AI can predict future trends and customer behaviors, helping you make informed decisions. For example, AI can forecast which products are likely to sell well during a particular season, allowing you to adjust your marketing and inventory strategies accordingly.

***

Let's look at a real-world example.

> A mid-sized e-commerce business specializing in home decor decided to implement AI to optimize their digital marketing strategy. They used Optimove for customer segmentation and Jasper for personalized email campaigns. The strategy involved analyzing customer purchase history to create detailed segments and then targeting these segments with personalized offers. The results were impressive. They saw a 25% increase in email open rates and a 30% boost in sales.

The key takeaway is that AI can significantly enhance the effectiveness of your marketing efforts by providing deeper insights and enabling more personalized interactions.

***

However, integrating AI into your digital marketing isn't without challenges. Data privacy and security are major concerns. With AI processing vast amounts of customer data, ensuring this data is secure and used ethically is paramount. Aligning AI tools with your business goals is another consideration. It's easy to get caught up in the latest technology, but you need to ensure that the AI tools you choose align with your overall strategy. Cost is another factor. While AI tools can provide a strong return on investment, the initial implementation can be expensive. Finally, there's the need for training and upskilling. Your team will need to understand how to use AI tools effectively, which might require ongoing training and development.

Implementing Chatbots for Customer Engagement

Imagine having a customer service representative that never sleeps, always provides instant responses, and can manage multiple interactions simultaneously. That's what chatbots bring to the table. Chatbots are automated programs designed to interact with users, mimicking human conversation. There are two main types: rule-based and AI-driven. Rule-based chatbots follow predefined scripts, while AI-driven chatbots use natural language processing (NLP) to understand and respond to user queries. These virtual assistants are versatile, serving roles in customer service, marketing, and even sales. They can answer FAQs, guide users through product selections, and provide personalized recommendations. The benefits are clear: 24/7 availability, instant responses, and the ability to handle numerous interactions without getting overwhelmed.

Setting up a chatbot for your business doesn't have to be a daunting task. Start by choosing the right platform. Options like Tidio, Drift, and Intercom offer user-friendly interfaces and robust features. Once you've selected a platform, design the chatbot's conversation flow. This involves mapping out potential user queries and the corresponding responses. Think of it as creating a decision tree. Integrating the chatbot with your website or social media channels is the next step. Most platforms provide easy-to-follow instructions for embedding the chatbot on your site or linking it to your social media profiles. Finally, test the chatbot for functionality and user experience. Run multiple scenarios to ensure it responds accurately and efficiently. Make adjustments as needed to refine its performance.

Designing an effective chatbot requires attention to detail. Start with natural language processing (NLP). This technology allows the chatbot to understand and interpret user queries accurately. Personalize interactions by using the user's name and tailoring responses based on their history with your brand. Clear and concise responses are necessary. Avoid long-winded answers that can confuse users. Instead, provide direct and relevant information. Another best practice is ensuring a smooth handoff to human agents when needed. While chatbots are powerful, they can't handle every situation. Make it easy for users to escalate issues to a human representative if the chatbot can't provide a satisfactory answer.

Measuring the performance of your chatbot is essential for continuous improvement. Key metrics to track include user engagement metrics like the number of interactions and session duration. These metrics help you understand how often and for how long users are engaging with the chatbot. Customer satisfaction scores provide insights into the quality of interactions. You can gather this data through post-interaction surveys. Conversion rates from chatbot interactions are another vital metric. Track how many users complete a desired action, like signing up for a newsletter or making a purchase, after interacting with the chatbot. Use analytics tools like Botanalytics and Chatbase to gather and analyze this data, helping you make informed decisions and optimizations.

Personalizing Marketing with AI

Personalization in marketing is all about tailoring your messages and offers to individual customers. Think of it as the digital equivalent of a shopkeeper who knows each customer by name and remembers their favorite products. This level of personalization can significantly improve the customer experience and increase engagement. When customers feel that a brand understands and values them, they're more likely to interact and convert. AI plays a important role in this by analyzing vast amounts of customer data to generate insights that help craft personalized marketing strategies. For example, personalized email campaigns that recommend products based on past purchases or browsing behavior can drive higher engagement and sales.

AI-driven tools are revolutionizing how we achieve this level of personalization. Dynamic content generation tools like Persado and Phrasee use AI to create personalized marketing messages that resonate with individual customers. These tools analyze data to understand what type of content works best for different segments, ensuring that each message is as effective as possible. Recommendation engines, like the ones used by Amazon, analyze user behavior to suggest products that customers are likely to be interested in. Personalized email marketing platforms such as Mailchimp and Sendinblue leverage AI to tailor email content and send times based on individual user data. Additionally, customer segmentation and targeting tools like Segment and Optimove allow marketers to create detailed customer segments and target them with personalized offers.

Implementing AI-driven personalization strategies starts with collecting and analyzing customer data. This data can come from various sources, including website interactions, purchase history, and social media activity. Once you have the data, the next step is to create detailed customer segments. These segments should be based on factors like demographics, behavior, and preferences. With these segments in place, you can use AI tools to personalize content and offers for each group. For instance, you might use AI to send personalized email offers to customers who have shown interest in a particular product category. AI can also automate this personalization, ensuring that each customer receives the most relevant content without manual intervention.

***

Consider this case study.

> A fashion retailer that successfully used AI for personalized marketing by using tools like Optimove for customer segmentation and Mailchimp for personalized email campaigns. By analyzing customer purchase history and browsing behavior, they created detailed segments and targeted these segments with personalized product recommendations and exclusive offers. The results were impressive: a 20% increase in email open rates and a 25% boost in sales.

The key takeaway from this case study is that AI-driven personalization can lead to higher engagement and conversion rates by making each customer feel valued and understood.

***

Using Machine Learning to Optimize Campaigns

Machine learning might sound like something out of a tech lab, but it's becoming a vital tool in digital marketing. At its core, machine learning involves algorithms that learn from data, identifying patterns and making decisions with minimal human intervention. Think about how Netflix recommends shows based on your viewing history, that's machine learning in action. In the context of marketing, machine learning can help optimize campaigns by analyzing vast amounts of data to predict outcomes, identify trends, and automate processes. For example, it can determine the best times to send emails or the most effective ad placements.

One of the most exciting applications of machine learning in marketing is campaign optimization. Imagine running a PPC campaign and needing to adjust your bids in real-time based on performance. Machine learning algorithms can handle this effortlessly. They analyze data from past campaigns to predict which keywords will perform best, adjusting bids dynamically to maximize ROI. Additionally, machine learning can optimize content delivery by analyzing user behavior to determine the most engaging content formats and topics for different audience segments. This ensures that your marketing messages are always relevant and timely, increasing the likelihood of engagement and conversion.

Several tools utilize machine learning to help marketers optimize their campaigns. Google Ads uses machine learning to recommend bid adjustments and identify high-performing keywords. Another powerful tool is HubSpot, which leverages machine learning to personalize content and automate marketing workflows. For email marketing, platforms like Mailchimp use machine learning to optimize send times and personalize email content based on user behavior. These tools simplify the complex process of campaign management, allowing you to focus on strategy while the algorithms handle the heavy lifting.

***

Consider a real-world example.

> A retail company that successfully used machine learning to optimize its marketing campaigns. They were struggling with high customer churn rates and ineffective email campaigns. By integrating machine learning tools like Optimove, they analyzed customer behavior and segmented their audience into distinct groups. Each segment received personalized email campaigns tailored to their preferences and past interactions. The result was a 15% increase in customer retention and a 20% boost in email open rates.

This case highlights how machine learning can turn around underperforming campaigns by providing actionable insights and enabling precise targeting.

***

While machine learning offers immense potential, there are challenges to consider. High-quality data is required for effective machine learning outcomes. Poor data quality can lead to inaccurate predictions and suboptimal performance. Additionally, the initial setup and integration of machine learning tools can be resource-intensive, requiring both time and financial investment. Furthermore, there's the need to continuously monitor and adjust the algorithms to ensure they align with your evolving marketing goals. Despite these challenges, the benefits of using machine learning for campaign optimization far outweigh the drawbacks, making it a valuable addition to your digital marketing toolkit.

Voice Search Optimization

Voice search is rapidly becoming a staple in how consumers seek information online. With the rise of smart speakers like Amazon's Alexa, Google Home, and Apple's Siri, more people are using voice commands to search for products, services, and answers. In fact, it's estimated that by 2024, nearly half of all online searches will be voice-based. This shift means that optimizing your content for voice search is no longer optional; it's a necessity. Voice search queries are typically longer and more conversational than typed searches, making it essential to adapt your content strategy accordingly.

Optimizing content for voice search starts with understanding how people speak. Unlike typed searches, voice queries often use natural language and complete sentences. Concentrate on long-tail keywords and phrases that have a natural, conversational tone. For instance, instead of targeting the keyword "best coffee shop," optimize for "What's the best coffee shop near me?" FAQs and blog posts that answer specific questions can be incredibly effective. Structure your content to provide clear, concise answers to common questions your audience might ask. This approach not only increases your chances of appearing in voice search results but also enhances the overall user experience.

From a technical standpoint, optimizing your website for voice search involves several key considerations. First, ensure your site is mobile-friendly. Most voice searches are conducted on mobile devices, so your site needs to load quickly and be easy to navigate. Page speed is crucial; use tools like Google Page Speed Insights to identify and fix any issues. Implementing structured data or schema markup can help search engines understand the context of your content, making it more likely to appear in rich snippets or featured snippets, prime real estate for voice search results. Additionally, secure your site with HTTPS, as search engines prioritize secure websites.

Measuring the effectiveness of your voice search optimization efforts requires a different approach than traditional SEO. Start by tracking the performance of your long-tail keywords and question-based queries using tools like Google Search Console. Monitor changes in organic traffic, especially from mobile devices. Use analytics to see if there's an increase in the number of users finding your content through voice search. Pay attention to metrics like bounce rate and session duration to gauge user engagement. Tools like SEMrush and Ahrefs can also provide insights into how your content is performing in voice search results, helping you refine your strategy for better outcomes.

Augmented Reality (AR) and Virtual Reality (VR) in Marketing

Imagine stepping into a virtual showroom from the comfort of your living room or seeing how that new sofa would look in your space without lifting a finger. That's the magic of Augmented Reality (AR) and Virtual Reality (VR). AR overlays digital elements onto the real world through devices like smartphones and AR glasses. VR, on the other hand, immerses users in a completely virtual environment using headsets like Oculus Rift or HTC Vive. Both technologies hold immense potential in digital marketing, transforming how customers interact with brands.

AR can significantly enhance marketing efforts by making products more interactive. For instance, beauty brands use AR to let customers try on makeup virtually through their smartphones. Home improvement stores offer AR apps that allow users to visualize how different paint colors or furniture pieces will look in their homes. This interactive experience not only engages customers but also helps them make more informed purchasing decisions, reducing return rates and increasing customer satisfaction. Additionally, AR can be used for gamification in marketing campaigns, creating engaging and shareable experiences that drive brand awareness.

VR offers a different kind of immersion. Imagine a travel agency using VR to give potential customers a virtual tour of a tropical resort. By experiencing the lush landscapes and luxurious amenities firsthand, customers are more likely to book an actual trip. Automotive companies are also leveraging VR to offer virtual test drives, allowing potential buyers to experience driving a car without stepping into a dealership. This not only creates a memorable experience but also helps in building an emotional connection with the brand. Moreover, VR can be used for virtual events and showrooms, providing an immersive experience for product launches and exhibitions.

Integrating AR and VR into your marketing strategy involves several practical steps. Start by identifying the right use for your business. Consider how AR or VR can solve a problem or enhance the customer experience. Next, choose the right technology and platform. There are numerous AR and VR development platforms available, such as Unity for VR and ARKit for iOS-based AR applications. Collaborate with developers to create a seamless and engaging experience. Once your AR or VR application is ready, promote it through your existing marketing channels. Educate your audience on how to use the technology and highlight the benefits. Finally, gather feedback and analyze the data to refine and improve the experience.

The Future of AI in Digital Marketing

AI in digital marketing is evolving rapidly, and keeping up with the latest trends can feel like chasing a moving target. One of the most exciting trends is AI-driven content creation. Tools like Jasper and Writer are revolutionizing how content is produced, allowing marketers to generate high-quality articles, social media posts, and even video scripts with minimal effort. These tools analyze audience preferences and optimize content for maximum engagement. Voice search optimization and smart assistants are also gaining traction. As more people use devices like Alexa and Google Assistant to search online, optimizing content for voice search is becoming mandatory.

Predictive analytics is another game changer. By analyzing historical data, AI can predict future trends and customer behaviors, allowing marketers to make proactive decisions. Imagine knowing which products will be in high demand next season or which marketing channels will yield the best ROI. AI in programmatic advertising is streamlining the ad-buying process. Algorithms automatically purchase ad space based on real-time data, ensuring that ads reach the right audience at the right time. This level of precision reduces wasted ad spend and increases campaign effectiveness.

Emerging AI technologies are poised to make an even more significant impact. Augmented reality (AR) and virtual reality (VR) are becoming more accessible, offering immersive experiences that can transform customer engagement. For instance, AR can allow customers to visualize products in their own space before making a purchase, while VR can offer virtual tours of properties or vacation destinations. AI-powered video content analysis is another exciting development. These tools can analyze video content to identify key themes, emotions, and audience engagement, helping marketers optimize their video strategies. Advanced natural language processing (NLP) is making chatbots and virtual assistants more intuitive and responsive, enhancing customer interactions. AI-driven influencer marketing platforms are also emerging, helping brands identify the most effective influencers for their campaigns based on data analytics rather than guesswork.

Preparing for these AI advancements requires a proactive approach. Staying updated with AI trends and innovations is a must. Regularly reading industry blogs, attending webinars, and participating in conferences can help you stay ahead of the curve. Investing in AI training and education for your marketing team ensures they have the skills needed to leverage these technologies effectively. Collaborating with AI technology providers can also provide valuable insights and access to cutting-edge tools. Creating a flexible and adaptive marketing strategy allows you to pivot quickly as new technologies emerge, ensuring you can capitalize on the latest advancements.

However, integrating AI into your marketing strategy brings ethical considerations. Ensuring transparency and accountability in your AI applications is essential. Customers should know when they're interacting with AI and how their data is used. Addressing biases in AI algorithms is also important. AI systems can inadvertently perpetuate existing biases, leading to unfair outcomes. Regularly auditing your AI systems and making necessary adjustments can mitigate these risks. Protecting customer data privacy is another key concern. Implement robust data security measures and comply with relevant regulations to build trust with your customers. Building trust is paramount. Transparent communication about how AI is used and how it benefits customers can foster a positive perception and encourage engagement.

Emerging Technologies to Watch

The digital marketing landscape is constantly evolving, and staying ahead means keeping an eye on emerging technologies that can revolutionize your strategies. Let's explore some of the most promising technologies that are set to redefine digital marketing.

Blockchain technology goes beyond serving as the foundation for cryptocurrencies like Bitcoin. In digital marketing, it has the potential to enhance transparency and trust, especially in advertising. Imagine a world where every ad impression and click is recorded on a blockchain, ensuring that all transactions are transparent and fraud is minimized. Blockchain can also improve data security and privacy by decentralizing data storage, making it harder for hackers to access sensitive information. Moreover, it enables secure and transparent transactions, which is particularly beneficial for programmatic advertising.

The Internet of Things (IoT) is another game-changer. IoT refers to the network of interconnected devices that collect and exchange data in real time. For marketers, this means access to unprecedented amounts of customer data. Imagine being able to collect real-time data from connected devices like smart fridges, wearable fitness trackers, and smart home assistants. This data can be used to personalize marketing messages and enhance the customer experience. For instance, a retailer can send personalized offers to a customer's smartphone based on their shopping habits recorded by a smart fridge. In retail marketing, IoT has been used to create more personalized and timely promotions, leading to higher customer satisfaction and increased sales.

5G connectivity is set to revolutionize digital marketing by providing faster and more reliable internet connections. This enhanced connectivity allows for the seamless integration of advanced technologies like AR, VR, and IoT. For mobile marketing, 5G means better user experiences with faster load times and higher-quality content. Consider a marketing initiative leveraging the capabilities of 5G to fuel an AR-driven shopping journey within a mobile application. This case study revealed that the implementation of a 5G-enhanced immersive marketing strategy led to increased user engagement with the brand, alongside a higher tendency for making purchases. These findings underscore the significant impact that 5G technology can have on enhancing customer interaction and driving sales.

Extended reality (XR), which encompasses AR, VR, and mixed reality, is another exciting frontier. These technologies offer new ways to engage with customers, providing immersive experiences that traditional media cannot match. For example, a furniture retailer could use AR to allow customers to visualize how a piece of furniture would look in their home, or a travel company could offer VR tours of exotic destinations. These immersive experiences can significantly enhance customer engagement and drive sales.

As we wrap up this chapter, it's clear that emerging technologies hold immense potential to transform digital marketing. From blockchain's transparency to IoT's data insights, 5G's speed, and XR's immersive experiences, these technologies are not just futuristic concepts but practical tools that can enhance your marketing strategy. Up next, we'll dive into real-world case studies and practical applications to bring these concepts to life.

Chapter Nine

Real-World Case Studies and Practical Applications

Ever felt like you're spinning your wheels with digital marketing? You're not alone. The best way to learn is often through real-world examples, where you can see what worked and what didn't. Let's dive into some case studies of the strategies previously discussed that turned the tide for struggling businesses. This isn't just theory; it's actionable insights you can apply to your own efforts.

Case Study: Successful SEO Campaigns

Meet "Eco-Friendly Living," a mid-sized e-commerce store specializing in sustainable household products. Despite having a fantastic range of eco-friendly goods, the company struggled with visibility online. They were stuck on the second or third page of Google search results, which, as you know, is virtually invisible. Their initial SEO issues included low organic traffic and poor rankings for key search terms. Their goal was clear: boost organic traffic, improve search engine rankings, and ultimately drive more sales through better online visibility.

The first step was comprehensive keyword research and selection. The team used tools like Google Keyword Planner and Ahrefs to identify high-volume, low-competition keywords relevant to their niche. They discovered that while broad terms like "eco-friendly products" were too competitive, long-tail keywords like "sustainable kitchen supplies" had significant search volume but less competition. This insight was crucial for targeting the right audience without getting lost in the noise.

Next came on-page optimization. This involved revamping title tags, meta descriptions, and header tags across the site. For instance, the title tag for their main page was changed from a generic "Eco-Friendly Store" to a more targeted "Buy Eco-Friendly Kitchen Supplies | Eco-Friendly Living." Meta descriptions were crafted to include primary keywords naturally, and header tags were used to structure content better. These changes made the site more appealing to search engines and improved user experience.

Off-page strategies were also pivotal. Building high-quality backlinks was a priority. The company engaged in guest blogging on reputable eco-friendly and sustainability blogs, which not only provided valuable backlinks but also positioned them as a thought leader in their niche. They also participated in industry forums and Q&A sites like Quora, answering questions related to sustainable living and linking back to their website. This not only drove traffic but also built domain authority.

Technical SEO improvements were another focus area. The website underwent a thorough audit using tools like SEMrush and Google Search Console. Issues such as slow page load times and poor mobile responsiveness were identified and addressed. Images were compressed, unnecessary plugins were removed, and the site was optimized for mobile users. These changes led to a significant improvement in user experience, which in turn positively impacted SEO rankings.

The results were impressive. Within six months, Eco-Friendly Living saw a 150% increase in organic traffic. Their search engine rankings for target keywords improved dramatically, with many keywords moving from the third page to the first. Conversion rates and leads generated from organic search also saw a notable boost, contributing to a 25% increase in overall sales. The site's performance metrics, such as bounce rate and average session duration, improved, indicating a better user experience.

Several key takeaways emerged from this campaign. First, continuous monitoring and optimization are crucial. SEO isn't a one-and-done task; it requires ongoing effort to maintain and improve rankings. High-quality content is another cornerstone of successful SEO. Informative, engaging content not only attracts visitors but also encourages other sites to link to yours. Technical SEO improvements, such as site speed and mobile optimization, have a significant impact on user experience and, consequently, on SEO performance. Finally, building high-quality backlinks remains one of the most effective ways to improve domain authority and search engine rankings.

By focusing on these strategies, you can significantly improve your SEO performance, driving more organic traffic and increasing your chances of converting visitors into customers.

Case Study: Effective Social Media Strategies

FitLife Apparel, a trendy athleisure brand targeting millennials and Gen Z. The company had a solid product line but struggled with its social media presence. Despite having accounts on major platforms like Instagram, Facebook, and Twitter (X), engagement was low, and the follower count was stagnant. Their primary audience was active, fashion-conscious young adults, but the brand's posts weren't resonating. The main issues included low engagement rates, lack of followers, and a general sense that their social media content wasn't hitting the mark. Their goal? To boost brand awareness, increase engagement, and drive sales through a revamped social media strategy.

The first order of business was platform selection and audience targeting. FitLife Apparel initially spread its efforts too thin across too many platforms. They decided to focus on Instagram and TikTok, where their target audience was most active. Instagram offered a visually-rich platform perfect for showcasing their stylish apparel, while TikTok provided a way to engage with trends and challenges popular among younger audiences. They used Instagram's audience insights and TikTok's analytics to identify the demographics and interests of their followers, allowing them to tailor content more effectively.

Content creation and planning were the next steps. FitLife Apparel decided to overhaul their content strategy, focusing on high-quality visuals, engaging videos, and regular stories. They hired a professional photographer to capture their products in action, showcasing the versatility and style of their athleisure line. User-generated content also played a significant role; they encouraged customers to share photos wearing FitLife products, which the brand then reposted. This not only provided fresh content but also built a sense of community. On TikTok, they participated in trending challenges and created short, engaging videos that highlighted the brand's fun and energetic vibe.

Engaging with the audience was another area where FitLife Apparel needed improvement. They started actively responding to comments, liking user posts, and hosting live Q&A sessions. These live sessions allowed followers to ask questions about the products, get style tips, and even see behind-the-scenes footage of new collections. This direct interaction made followers feel more connected to the brand, fostering a loyal community. They also ran polls and quizzes on Instagram Stories to encourage interaction and gather feedback on what their audience wanted to see.

Social media advertising was the final piece of the puzzle. FitLife Apparel allocated a budget specifically for targeted ads on Instagram and TikTok. They created eye-catching ads showcasing best-selling items and new arrivals, targeting users based on their interests, behaviors, and demographics. They also used retargeting ads to reach people who had visited their website but hadn't made a purchase. This approach ensured that their ads were seen by the right people, maximizing the return on investment.

The results were nothing short of impressive. Within three months, FitLife Apparel saw a 200% increase in Instagram followers and a 150% increase in TikTok followers. Engagement rates soared, with likes, comments, and shares tripling across both platforms. Their posts reached a broader audience, resulting in higher impressions and enhanced brand visibility. Most importantly, these efforts translated into tangible business results. Sales and lead generation improved significantly, with a 30% increase in online sales attributed directly to social media traffic.

Several key takeaways emerged from this campaign. Understanding your target audience is critical. Knowing where they spend their time online and what content they engage with allows you to tailor your strategy effectively. Consistent and engaging content keeps your audience interested and coming back for more. Utilizing social media advertising can boost visibility and drive conversions, especially when you target the right audience. Active engagement with your audience builds a sense of community and loyalty, which can significantly impact your brand's success.

Case Study: High-Impact Content Marketing

TechSavvy Solutions, a B2B company specializing in software solutions for small businesses. Despite having innovative products, they struggled to capture the attention of their target market. Their content marketing efforts were sporadic, leading to low engagement and a lack of brand authority. Their main issues included a lack of a cohesive content strategy and minimal user engagement. Their goal was to establish themselves as industry leaders and generate quality leads through a robust content marketing campaign.

The first step was developing a comprehensive content marketing plan. TechSavvy Solutions started by identifying their target audience's pain points and interests. They conducted surveys and social media polls to gather insights directly from their potential customers. This research helped them create detailed buyer personas, which were instrumental in crafting relevant content. They also set clear objectives, such as increasing website traffic by 30% within six months and generating 100 new leads per month.

Creating high-quality, valuable content became the cornerstone of their strategy. They decided to focus on a mix of blog posts, videos, and infographics. Each piece of content was designed to educate and inform, offering practical solutions to common problems faced by small businesses. For example, they published blog posts on topics like "Top 10 Tips for Streamlining Your Small Business Operations" and "How to Choose the Right Software for Your Business Needs." They also created in-depth video tutorials and visually appealing infographics that broke down complex concepts into easy-to-understand visuals.

Content distribution and promotion were equally important. They leveraged social media platforms like LinkedIn and Twitter (X) to share their content, targeting industry-specific groups and hashtags to maximize reach. Email newsletters were another key channel. They built a high-quality email list by offering valuable lead magnets, such as free eBooks and whitepapers, in exchange for email sign-ups. Their newsletters featured a mix of blog excerpts, video links, and exclusive tips, driving traffic back to their website. They also repurposed content into different formats to reach a wider audience. For instance, a popular blog post turned into a video, ensuring the content had multiple touchpoints.

The results were impressive. Within six months, TechSavvy Solutions saw a 40% increase in website traffic, far exceeding their initial goal. User engagement also improved, with the average time spent on their site increasing by 25%. Their content was widely shared, generating valuable backlinks that boosted their search engine rankings. They established themselves as thought leaders in their industry, which was reflected in the quality of leads they attracted. The number of leads generated per month doubled, leading to a significant increase in conversions and sales.

Several key takeaways emerged from this campaign. First, a well-defined content strategy is pivotal. Knowing your audience and setting clear objectives provides direction and focus. High-quality, valuable content is the foundation of successful content marketing. It not only attracts visitors but also keeps them engaged and coming back for more. Effective content distribution and promotion ensure your content reaches the right people. Leveraging multiple channels and repurposing content maximizes its impact. Finally, the value of repurposing content cannot be overstated. It allows you to extend the life of your content and reach a broader audience without constantly creating new material.

Case Study: Email Campaigns that Convert

GreenGardens, a small business specializing in organic gardening supplies. They had a fantastic product line, but their email marketing was falling flat. Low open rates and high unsubscribe rates plagued their campaigns, leaving them frustrated. Their primary goal was to engage their audience better, reduce unsubscribe rates, and drive more sales through email marketing. They needed a strategy overhaul to turn things around.

The first step was building a high-quality email list. GreenGardens moved away from buying email lists and focused on organic growth. They created lead magnets such as free eBooks on organic gardening tips, exclusive discounts, and early access to new products. These incentives were promoted on their website and social media channels, encouraging visitors to sign up. This approach ensured that their email list was filled with people genuinely interested in their products, leading to higher engagement.

Next, they crafted compelling subject lines and email content. They realized that their previous subject lines were too generic and failed to grab attention. They began using A/B testing to experiment with different subject lines, focusing on personalization and urgency. For instance, subject lines like "Unlock Exclusive Tips for Your Garden" or "Limited-Time Offer: Get 20% Off Organic Seeds" performed much better. The email content also saw a revamp, shifting from purely promotional to a mix of valuable content and offers. They included gardening tips, customer testimonials, and user-generated content, making the emails more engaging and less salesy.

Segmenting the email list was another key. Instead of sending the same email to everyone, GreenGardens segmented their list based on customer behavior and preferences. They created segments for new subscribers, repeat customers, and inactive subscribers. Each segment received tailored content. New subscribers got a welcome series with information about the brand and beginner gardening tips. Repeat customers received loyalty rewards and exclusive offers, while inactive subscribers were re-engaged with special discounts and surveys to understand their needs better.

Conducting A/B testing became a regular practice. They tested different elements of their emails, such as send times, call-to-action buttons, and content formats. For example, they found that emails sent on Tuesday mornings had higher open rates compared to those sent on Fridays. They also discovered that using buttons for call-to-actions instead of text links increased click-through rates. These insights allowed them to refine their strategy continuously, optimizing for better performance.

The results were remarkable. GreenGardens saw a 50% increase in open rates and a 40% boost in click-through rates. Engagement skyrocketed, with more subscribers interacting with their emails and visiting their website. Unsubscribe rates dropped significantly, indicating that their content was resonating with their audience. Most importantly, customer retention and loyalty improved, leading to a 25% increase in repeat purchases. The quality of their email list improved, making their campaigns more effective and efficient.

Several key takeaways emerged from this campaign. Building a high-quality email list with lead magnets ensures that your audience is genuinely interested in your content. Crafting compelling subject lines and email content grabs attention and keeps subscribers engaged. Segmenting your email list allows for personalized and relevant communication, increasing the likelihood of conversions. Regular A/B testing helps optimize performance by identifying what works best for your audience. These strategies can transform your email marketing efforts, driving higher engagement and conversions.

Case Study: Leveraging AI for Marketing Success

BrightHome, specializing in home decor and furniture. Despite having a wide range of stylish products, struggled to convert casual browsers into loyal customers. That's where AI comes in. BrightHome decided to leverage AI for personalized product recommendations, aiming to boost sales and customer satisfaction.

The campaign started with the implementation of machine learning algorithms and recommendation engines. They used AI tools like Dynamic Yield and Salesforce Einstein to analyze customer data and generate personalized product suggestions. The objective was clear: enhance the shopping experience, increase sales, and improve customer satisfaction. Within six months, BrightHome saw a 35% increase in sales and a significant uptick in customer satisfaction scores.

The AI implementation process was meticulous. It began with data collection and analysis. BrightHome gathered data from various touchpoints, including website interactions, purchase history, and customer reviews. This data was then fed into machine learning models to train them. The AI tools analyzed patterns and behaviors to predict what products individual customers might be interested in. Once the models were trained, they were deployed across the website and email campaigns, delivering personalized recommendations in real-time. Continuous optimization was key. The AI models were regularly updated with new data, ensuring they stayed accurate and relevant.

Challenges were inevitable, but they were tackled head-on. Data privacy and security were major concerns. BrightHome ensured compliance with GDPR and other data protection regulations by implementing robust security measures and obtaining customer consent for data usage. Ensuring algorithm accuracy was another hurdle. Initial recommendations were sometimes off the mark, leading to customer frustration. The team addressed this by fine-tuning the algorithms and incorporating feedback loops to improve accuracy over time.

Several key takeaways emerged from this AI-driven campaign. High-quality data is crucial for training AI models effectively. Garbage in, garbage out, as they say. The better the data, the more accurate the AI's predictions. Balancing automation with human oversight is also essential. While AI can handle vast amounts of data and make quick decisions, human oversight ensures that the recommendations align with the brand's values and customer expectations. Continuous monitoring and adjustment of AI systems are necessary. AI isn't a set-it-and-forget-it solution. Regular updates and refinements keep the models performing at their best.

For instance, BrightHome found that customers who browsed for living room furniture were often interested in decor items like throw pillows and rugs. By integrating this insight, the AI started recommending complementary products, leading to higher average order values. They also implemented A/B testing to compare the performance of AI-driven recommendations against traditional methods. The AI-driven approach consistently outperformed, with higher engagement and conversion rates.

BrightHome's success with AI illustrates how powerful these technologies can be when implemented thoughtfully. By focusing on high-quality data, ensuring robust security, and maintaining a balance between automation and human oversight, businesses can achieve remarkable results. The insights gained from this campaign are actionable and can be applied to any business looking to leverage AI for marketing success.

Lessons Learned from Digital Marketing Failures

You've heard success stories, but what about the times when things didn't go as planned? Understanding why digital marketing campaigns fail can save you from making the same mistakes. Common pitfalls include unclear goals, a poor grasp of the target audience, inadequate budget allocation, and a failure to measure and analyze performance. Without clear objectives, your campaigns lack direction. Not understanding your audience can make your messages fall flat. Skimping on budget often leads to subpar results, and neglecting performance metrics means you're flying blind. Let's dive into some real-world examples to see how these issues play out.

Healthy Bites, a small organic snack company. They embarked on an SEO campaign to boost online visibility. The initial strategies included keyword stuffing and producing low-quality content stuffed with keywords. These tactics might have worked a decade ago, but Google's algorithms have evolved. The results were disappointing. Organic traffic barely budged, and their search rankings remained stagnant.

The lesson here is clear: quality trumps quantity. Focus on creating valuable content that addresses your audience's needs and avoid black-hat tactics that can get you penalized. The company learned to prioritize user experience and content relevance, leading to a more effective SEO strategy down the line.

Trendy Threads, a fashion retailer that launched a social media campaign to increase brand awareness. They chose Instagram and Facebook, but the campaign fell flat. The content was sporadic, with no consistent posting schedule. Engagement was low because the posts didn't resonate with their target audience, young adults interested in fashion trends. The lack of planning and audience understanding were major issues. From this failure, Trendy Threads learned the importance of consistent, engaging content and the need to understand their audience's preferences. They revamped their strategy, focusing on high-quality visuals and regular posts, which eventually led to better engagement and increased followers.

Several key lessons emerge from these failures. First, always set clear, achievable goals. Without them, your efforts lack focus and direction. Understand and target the right audience. Conduct thorough research to ensure your messages resonate. Budget effectively; cutting corners can lead to poor results. Finally, continuously measure and optimize performance. Use analytics tools to track your progress and make data-driven decisions. By learning from these mistakes, you can avoid common pitfalls and set your digital marketing campaigns on the path to success.

Chapter Ten

Continuous Learning and Adaptation

S taying ahead in the game of digital marketing often feels like trying to hit a moving target. You can master one concept today, and by tomorrow, there's a new trend or tool you need to know about. This constant evolution isn't just a nuisance, it's the key factor of effective marketing strategies. But how do you keep up without feeling overwhelmed? The secret lies in continuous learning and adaptation.

Staying Updated with Digital Marketing Trends

Digital marketing is a rapidly evolving field. Every day brings new tools, technologies, and trends that can either make or break your strategy. Staying current isn't just an option; it's a necessity. The digital landscape changes swiftly, and what worked yesterday might not work tomorrow. Adapting to these changes gives you a competitive edge, ensuring you're not left behind. When you stay updated, you're better positioned to meet changing customer expectations. Consumers today are more informed and connected than ever, and they expect businesses to keep up. Leveraging new tools and technologies can set you apart, making your campaigns more effective and efficient.

Reliable sources are important for staying informed about the latest trends and updates in digital marketing. Industry blogs and websites like Moz, HubSpot, and Search Engine Journal are treasure troves of information. They offer insights, updates, and practical tips you can implement immediately. Subscribing to digital marketing newsletters, such as

The Moz Top 10 or Neil Patel's newsletter, ensures that the latest news and trends land directly in your inbox. Social media platforms are also invaluable. Twitter and LinkedIn groups are particularly useful for real-time updates and professional discussions. Podcasts and webinars provide deep dives into specific topics, allowing you to learn from industry experts without leaving your desk.

Attending industry events can be a game-changer. Conferences, seminars, and webinars offer networking opportunities that can lead to valuable collaborations. You get to learn from the best in the business, discovering new tools and technologies that can enhance your marketing efforts. Events like the Social Media Strategies Summit and the Adobe Summit are perfect examples. These events feature sessions led by industry leaders, offering insights into current and future trends. They're also great for hands-on learning, with workshops and roundtables that allow you to delve into specific topics.

Engaging with online communities is another effective way to stay updated. Platforms like LinkedIn groups, Reddit communities (e.g., r/digital_marketing), and industry-specific Slack channels are buzzing with discussions, tips, and news. These communities are gold mines for real-time advice and peer support. Participating in these forums not only keeps you informed but also allows you to share your knowledge, building your reputation as a leader. Contributing to Q&A platforms like Quora can also be beneficial. Answering questions helps you refine your understanding while showcasing your expertise to a broader audience.

Checklist: Staying Updated with Digital Marketing Trends

- **Subscribe to Industry Blogs and Websites**: Moz, HubSpot, Search Engine Journal

- **Sign Up for Newsletters**: The Moz Top 10, Neil Patel's newsletter

- **Follow on Social Media**: Twitter, LinkedIn groups

- **Listen to Podcasts and Attend Webinars**: Stay updated with in-depth discussions

- **Attend Industry Events**: Network, learn, and discover new tools

- **Engage with Online Communities**: Participate in LinkedIn groups, Reddit, Slack channels

- **Contribute to Q&A Platforms**: Enhance your knowledge and visibility on Quora

By incorporating these practices into your routine, you can stay ahead of the curve and ensure your digital marketing strategies remain effective and relevant.

Resources for Continuous Learning

Keeping up with digital marketing trends is one thing, but diving deep into the material requires a commitment to continuous learning. This means seeking out resources that provide you with in-depth knowledge and practical skills. Online courses and certifications are a great way to start. Google Analytics Academy offers courses that teach you everything from the basics to advanced analytics. These courses are free and provide a certification upon completion, making them perfect for both beginners and seasoned professionals looking to polish their skills.

HubSpot Academy is another fantastic resource. It offers a range of free courses on topics like inbound marketing, content marketing, and email marketing. The courses are well-structured and include quizzes and practical exercises to test your knowledge. For a more comprehensive learning experience, consider Coursera's Digital Marketing Specialization. This program, in partnership with the University of Illinois, covers everything from digital marketing analytics to social media marketing. It's more intensive and requires a time commitment, but the depth of knowledge you gain is invaluable.

SEMrush Academy is perfect for those who want to dive deep into SEO, PPC, and content marketing. The courses are taught by industry experts and cover advanced topics that can give you a competitive edge. They offer certifications that can enhance your resume and demonstrate your expertise to potential clients or employers.

Webinars and workshops offer practical insights and hands-on learning experiences. HubSpot's free webinars cover a broad range of topics, from inbound marketing to sales strategies. These sessions are led by industry experts and often include Q&A segments, allowing you to get specific questions answered. SEMrush also offers webinars that dive into advanced SEO and PPC techniques. These are perfect for those looking to take their skills to the next level.

Social Media Examiner's workshops are another excellent resource. They offer both virtual and in-person events that cover everything from social media strategy to content creation. These workshops are interactive, providing opportunities to apply what you've learned in real-time. Don't overlook local digital marketing meetups and events. These gatherings provide a casual environment to learn, share experiences, and network with like-minded professionals.

Mentorship and networking can significantly accelerate your growth in digital marketing. Finding a mentor through LinkedIn or industry associations can provide you with personalized guidance and support. A mentor can help you navigate challenges, offer advice based on their experiences, and introduce you to valuable contacts. Look for someone whose career path aligns with your goals and who has the expertise you seek.

Participating in industry-specific networking events can open doors to new opportunities. These events allow you to meet people who are facing similar challenges and can offer solutions you might not have considered. Networking isn't just about finding new clients or job opportunities; it's about building relationships that can support your growth and development over the long term.

Joining professional organizations like the American Marketing Association (AMA) can also be beneficial. These organizations offer resources, certifications, and networking opportunities that can help you stay ahead in the industry. Attending local marketing meetups is another great way to build your network. These events are often less formal and provide a platform to discuss trends, share tips, and collaborate on projects.

Adapting Your Strategy for Long-Term Success

Regularly reviewing and updating your digital marketing strategies is like maintaining a car. You don't just drive it forever without checking the oil or rotating the tires. To ensure your marketing efforts stay effective and relevant, conduct quarterly or annual strategy reviews. This involves diving into performance data and key metrics to see what's working and what's not. Look at your conversion rates, engagement metrics, and ROI. Are there areas where performance has dipped? Identify these weak spots and think about what could be improved. Maybe your email open rates have dropped, or perhaps your social media engagement isn't as high as it used to be. Based on these insights, adjust your strategies. This could mean anything from tweaking your content calendar to changing your SEO tactics.

Embracing a growth mindset is necessary in the world of digital marketing. This mindset involves being open to experimentation and innovation. Encourage a culture of continuous improvement within your team. This means testing new ideas and strategies without the fear of failure. Not every experiment will succeed, but each one will offer valuable lessons. Celebrate the successes and analyze the failures to understand what went wrong. Staying adaptable and flexible allows you to pivot quickly when new trends or tools emerge. For instance, if a new social media platform starts gaining traction, don't hesitate to explore its potential for your business.

Incorporating feedback and insights from various sources can significantly refine your strategies. Collect customer feedback through surveys and reviews. This can provide direct insights into what your audience likes or dislikes about your current approach. Additionally, hold regular team meetings to discuss these insights. Your team members interact with different aspects of your marketing efforts and can offer diverse perspectives. Use this feedback to improve customer experience. If multiple customers mention that your website is hard to navigate, it's time to consider a redesign. Involving stakeholders in strategy planning ensures that everyone is aligned and working towards common goals.

Leveraging the latest technology and tools can give your digital marketing efforts a significant boost. AI and machine learning tools, for instance, can analyze vast amounts of data more efficiently than humans ever could. These tools can identify patterns and trends that might not be immediately obvious, helping you make data-driven decisions. Implementing marketing automation platforms like Marketo or HubSpot can streamline your processes. These platforms can handle tasks like email campaigns, social media postings, and customer segmentation, freeing up your team to focus on more strategic activities. Adopting new social media management tools can enhance your ability to schedule posts, engage with your audience, and analyze performance all in one place. Exploring advanced analytics software provides deeper insights into your marketing metrics, helping you fine-tune your strategies for better results.

Regular strategy reviews, a growth mindset, incorporating feedback, and leveraging technology are all part of adapting your strategy for long-term success. By keeping these elements in mind, you can ensure your digital marketing efforts remain effective and relevant in an ever-changing landscape.

Conclusion

We've come a long way together. From the start, our goal was simple: to give you a complete guide to building a successful digital marketing strategy. Along the way, we've explored AI technologies, reviewed real-world examples, and made industry terms easy to understand. Now, let's bring everything together and look at what's next..

Throughout this book, we've covered a ton of ground. We began by laying a strong foundation in digital marketing, emphasizing the importance of understanding the basics and the digital marketing ecosystem. We then moved on to creating a digital marketing strategy, where we discussed setting SMART goals, identifying your target audience, and choosing the right channels. From there, we explored the depths of SEO, social media marketing, content marketing, and email marketing, providing you with actionable insights and strategies to excel in each area.

Next, we showcased the power of data analytics and AI in optimizing your marketing efforts. We took a deep dive into understanding user behavior, analyzing traffic sources, and leveraging machine learning. Finally, we wrapped up with real-world case studies and practical applications, showing you how to learn from both successes and failures.

Here are some key takeaways to keep in mind as you move forward:

- **Understand Your Audience**: Always start by knowing who your customers are. Use surveys, social media insights, and analytics to gather data and create detailed buyer personas.

- **Set Clear Goals**: Use the SMART framework to set specific, measurable, achievable, relevant, and time-bound goals. This will guide your efforts and help you stay focused.

- **Choose the Right Channels**: Evaluate different digital marketing channels and select those that align with your audience and goals. Don't spread yourself too thin; focus on where you can make the most impact.

- **Leverage Content Marketing**: Create high-quality, engaging content that addresses your audience's needs and pain points. Use a content calendar to stay organized and consistent.

- **Optimize for SEO**: Both on-page and off-page SEO are critical for improving your search engine rankings. Regularly update your content, build high-quality backlinks, and ensure your website is mobile-friendly and fast.

- **Utilize AI and Data Analytics**: Use AI tools for personalization, predictive analytics, and campaign optimization. Leverage data analytics to track performance, make data-driven decisions, and continuously refine your strategies.

- **Engage on Social Media**: Choose the right platforms for your audience, create engaging content, and actively interact with your followers. Use social media advertising to boost visibility and drive conversions.

- **Effective Email Marketing**: Build a high-quality email list, craft compelling subject lines, and personalize your content. Segment your audience and use A/B testing to optimize your campaigns.

Now, here's your call to action: Take the insights and strategies you've learned and start applying them to your own digital marketing efforts. Begin by setting clear goals and understanding your audience. Choose the right channels and create a content plan. Use SEO best practices to optimize your website, and leverage AI and data analytics to refine your campaigns. Engage with your audience on social media and run effective email marketing campaigns.

Remember, digital marketing is not a one-time effort. It's a continuous process of learning, adapting, and improving. Stay updated with the latest trends, experiment with new ideas, and don't be afraid to make mistakes. Every failure is a learning opportunity that brings you one step closer to success.

In closing, I want to leave you with this thought: Embrace the ever-evolving world of digital marketing. It's a dynamic field that offers endless opportunities for growth and innovation. With the right strategies and a commitment to continuous learning, you can achieve substantial success and create a profitable business.

You've got the tools and knowledge now. It's time to put them to use. Go out there, make an impact, and watch your business thrive. Thank you for allowing me to be part of your digital marketing journey. Here's to your success!

Keeping the Game Alive

Now you have everything you need to master digital marketing and build a profitable customer base, it's time to pass on your newfound knowledge and show other readers where they can find the same help.

Simply by leaving your honest opinion of this book on Amazon, you'll show other aspiring marketers where they can find the information they're looking for, and pass their passion for starting a business forward.

Thank you for your help. The spirit of marketing is kept alive when we pass on our knowledge – and you're helping us to do just that.

References

Adobe. (n.d.). *Digital marketing metrics your business should be using.* Retrieved from https://business.adobe.com/blog/basics/digital-marketing-metrics

Ahrefs. (n.d.). *15 SEO case studies you can learn from.* Retrieved from https://ahrefs.com/blog/seo-case-studies

Backlinko. (n.d.). *17 best keyword research tools for SEO [2024 reviews].* Retrieved from https://backlinko.com/keyword-research-tools

Bluecore. (n.d.). *10 best practices for A/B testing your email marketing.* Retrieved from https://www.bluecore.com/blog/email-marketing-a-b-testing

Brevo. (n.d.). *A guide to GDPR compliance for email marketers in 2023.* Retrieved from https://www.brevo.com/blog/gdpr-email-marketing

Digital Marketing Institute. (n.d.). *AI in digital marketing: The ultimate guide.* Retrieved from https://digitalmarketinginstitute.com/blog/ai-in-digital-marketing-the-ultimate-guide

Digital Marketing Institute. (n.d.). *AI-based marketing personalization: How machines can drive personalization in marketing.* Retrieved from https://www.marketingaiinstitute.com/blog/ai-based-marketing-personalization

Digital Marketing Institute. (n.d.). *What are the best AI marketing tools?* Retrieved from https://digitalmarketinginstitute.com/blog/what-are-the-best-ai-and-marketing-automation-tools

Forbes. (2020, July 2). *Building a brand: Why a strong digital presence matters.* Retrieved from https://www.forbes.com/councils/forbesagencycouncil/2020/07/02/building-a-brand-why-a-strong-digital-presence-matters

Fractl. (n.d.). *10 case studies that show the real impact of content marketing.* Retrieved from https://www.frac.tl/10-content-marketing-case-studies

HubSpot. (n.d.). *27 case study examples every marketer should see*. Retrieved from https
://blog.hubspot.com/marketing/case-study-examples

HubSpot. (n.d.). *How to create detailed buyer personas for your business*. Retrieved from
https://blog.hubspot.com/marketing/buyer-persona-research

HubSpot. (n.d.). *The 25 best content marketing tools in 2024*. Retrieved from https://b
log.hubspot.com/marketing/content-marketing-tools

Influencer Marketing Hub. (n.d.). *Top 15 digital marketing events for 2023*. Retrieved
from https://influencermarketinghub.com/digital-marketing-events

Instagram for Business. (n.d.). *HM success story*. Retrieved from https://business.instag
ram.com/success/hm

Intelligent. (n.d.). *The 10 best online marketing courses of 2023*. Retrieved from https://
www.intelligent.com/best-online-courses/digital-marketing-courses/

Jetpack. (n.d.). *6 best social media platforms for business marketing in 2024*. Retrieved
from https://jetpack.com/blog/best-social-media-platforms-for-business/

LearnCourses. (n.d.). *Case studies: Success stories of brands using AI-driven marketing
automation*. Medium. Retrieved from https://medium.com/@LearnCourses/case-st
udies-success-stories-of-brands-using-ai-driven-marketing-automation-88f7c39f8085

Marketer Interview. (n.d.). *8 key lessons learned from a failed digital marketing campaign*.
Retrieved from https://marketerinterview.com/8-key-lessons-learned-from-a-failed
-digital-marketing-campaign

Metricool. (n.d.). *Top digital marketing trends in 2023*. Retrieved from https://metric
ool.com/digital-marketing-trends/

MobiDev. (n.d.). *How machine learning can be used in marketing*. Retrieved from http
s://mobidev.biz/blog/how-machine-learning-improves-marketing-strategies

Porter Metrics. (n.d.). *Top 10 digital marketing KPIs that you track in 2023*. Retrieved
from https://portermetrics.com/en/articles/digital-marketing-kpis/

Propelrr. (n.d.). *Case studies about social media marketing and its impact*. Retrieved from
https://propelrr.com/blog/case-studies-about-social-media

S2W Media. (n.d.). *15 effective email marketing strategies for 2023*. Retrieved from htt
ps://www.s2wmedia.com/blogs/email-marketing-strategies

Sacred Heart University. (n.d.). *The importance of a digital marketing strategy in today's
world*.   Retrieved   from
https://www.sacredheart.edu/academics/colleges--schools/college-of-business--techn

ology/departments--schools/marketing/digital-marketing-blog/the-impor-tance-of-a-digital-marketing-strategy-in-todays-world/

Search Engine Journal. (n.d.). *How to create engaging social media content: 12 tips to boost your strategy.* Retrieved from https://www.searchenginejournal.com/create-engaging-social-media-content-tips/378521/

Search Engine Journal. (n.d.). *What is user experience? How design matters to SEO.* Retrieved from https://www.searchenginejournal.com/ux-design-seo/476959/

Semrush. (n.d.). *Google E-E-A-T: What it is & how it affects SEO.* Retrieved from https://www.semrush.com/blog/eeat/

Semrush. (n.d.). *Google Analytics traffic sources: An in-depth guide.* Retrieved from https://www.semrush.com/blog/traffic-sources-ga4/

Semrush. (n.d.). *How to set up GA4: A complete step-by-step guide (2024).* Retrieved from https://www.semrush.com/blog/how-to-set-up-google-analytics/

Semrush. (n.d.). *The ultimate guide to creating a content marketing strategy.* Retrieved from https://www.semrush.com/blog/content-marketing-strategy-guide/

Shopify. (2024). *How to build an email list: 12 winning strategies.* Retrieved from https://www.shopify.com/blog/build-email-list

Simplilearn. (n.d.). *The history and evolution of digital marketing.* Retrieved from https://www.simplilearn.com/history-and-evolution-of-digital-marketing-article

Smart Insights. (n.d.). *How to define SMART marketing objectives.* Retrieved from https://www.smartinsights.com/goal-setting-evaluation/goals-kpis/define-smart-marketing-objectives/

Sprinklr. (n.d.). *7 examples of social media strategies that work well.* Retrieved from https://www.sprinklr.com/blog/social-media-strategy-examples/

Sprout Social. (n.d.). *The social media metrics to track in 2024 (and why).* Retrieved from https://sproutsocial.com/insights/social-media-metrics/

Twilio. (n.d.). *9 best content calendar tools for omnichannel marketing.* Retrieved from https://www.twilio.com/en-us/blog/content-calendar-tools

USC Annenberg. (n.d.). *4 research methods for audience analysis.* Retrieved from https://communicationmgmt.usc.edu/blog/4-research-methods-for-audience-analysis/

WordStream. (n.d.). *12 biggest SEO trends to watch in 2024.* Retrieved from https://www.wordstream.com/blog/2024-seo-trends

Zapier. (n.d.). *The best heatmap software and session replay tools*. Retrieved from https://zapier.com/blog/best-session-replay-heatmap-software/

Zapier. (n.d.). *The 6 best chatbot builders in 2024*. Retrieved from https://zapier.com/blog/best-chatbot-builders/